# The Diversity Code

# The
# Diversity Code

Unlock the Secrets to Making Differences
Work in the Real World

**MICHELLE T. JOHNSON**

**AMACOM**

**AMERICAN MANAGEMENT ASSOCIATION**

New York • Atlanta • Brussels • Chicago • Mexico City • San Francisco
Shanghai • Tokyo • Toronto • Washington, D.C.

Bulk discounts available. For details visit:
www.amacombooks.org/go/specialsales
Or contact special sales:
Phone: 800-250-5308
E-mail: specialsls@amanet.org
View all the AMACOM titles at: www.amacombooks.org

This publication is designed to provide accurate and authoritative information in regard to the subject matter covered. It is sold with the understanding that the publisher is not engaged in rendering legal, accounting, or other professional service. If legal advice or other expert assistance is required, the services of a competent professional person should be sought.

Johnson, Michelle T.
    The diversity code : unlock the secrets to making differences work in the real world / Michelle T. Johnson.
        p. cm.
    Includes index.
    ISBN-13: 978-0-8144-1632-7 (pbk.)
    ISBN-10: 0-8144-1632-2 (pbk.)
    1. Diversity in the workplace. 2. Diversity in the workplace—United States. I. Title.
    HF5549.5.M5J653 2011
    658.3008—dc22                                                                 2010006681

About AMA
American Management Association (www.amanet.org) is a world leader in talent development, advancing the skills of individuals to drive business success. Our mission is to support the goals of individuals and organizations through a complete range of products and services, including classroom and virtual seminars, webcasts, webinars, podcasts, conferences, corporate and government solutions, business books, and research. AMA's approach to improving performance combines experiential learning—learning through doing—with opportunities for ongoing professional growth at every step of one's career journey.

Printing number
10 9 8 7 6 5 4 3 2 1

I was sent a quote recently that said that people will forget what you've said,
people will forget what you've done, but people will never forget how you made them feel.

This book is dedicated to all the friends I've met in the workplace
over the years who have made me feel bright and respected and valued
and appreciated and to the people who allowed me to give back that same gift.

# CONTENTS

# ACKNOWLEDGMENTS

My thanks go to God first, last, and in the cracks and crevices in between; my two Maries—my mother, Ethel Marie, and my grandmother, Cliffie Marie, who provided the foundation I stand upon daily; my best friend and rock Adrienne H. Bennett; all of my friends but *special* thanks to my dream team of girlfriends who provide laughter and steel-tipped boots to keep me on track, most notably Larrye J. Murrell, Joy A. Springfield, Cherry Muhanji, and Jessica Kerrigan; the entire Stites family (Mark, Leigh, Ashley, Emily, and Kathryne), who fed me enough to write ten books; my faithful, fluffy writing companions, Hilbert Ray and Henry Jay; my literary agent, Sha-Shana Crichton of Crichton & Associates; and my editor, Christina Parisi of AMACOM Books, for making all this possible.

Special thanks also to my immense spiritual community at Kansas City's Center for Spiritual Living, with particular loving gratitude to Ora Stafford, Judy Whitcraft, Mike Irwin, Mark Hayes, and Reverend Jarie Newsome.

And thanks to my creative muses who left this world way too soon but whose influences will forever inspire and nurture me—thank you, Gordon Parks, Luther Vandross, and Octavia Butler.

# The Diversity Code

# So What Is the Diversity Code, Anyway?

*Dear Diversity Diva:*

*What exactly is this book going to do for me that all the mandatory diversity seminars, workshops, and training sessions that I've been required to go to as a manager haven't already done? And what the devil makes you a "Diversity Diva" in the first place?*

*Signed,*
*Book Paid for on Credit Card*

What this book will do—differently from any other diversity talk you've ever had to sit through or diversity brochure you've been required to read— is tell it to you straight. I'm not going to sugarcoat diversity and make it palatable. I'm also not going to surround it with a political agenda or explain it in a way that makes it nothing more than sociological cough syrup.

As you read this book, you'll get mad at some things I say. Sometimes, you'll chuckle to yourself. But most important, you'll be spurred to start thinking a little differently, which is the key to managing diversity issues.

Giving you a list of do's or don'ts would be an exercise in futility, so I'm not going to do that. The women's magazine *Glamour* ends every issue with pictures of fashion do's and don'ts, based on pictures of real women walking around. Seeing a picture of someone looking like a hot mess indirectly tells you what not to wear.

That's great for a monthly magazine and particularly great for illustrating the changing winds of fashion. But diversity isn't so cut-and-dried. That's why I said that it's about thinking differently. When it comes to managing diversity issues, it becomes really important to think a little differently, because if you view the world differently, you show up in the world differently, which impacts how you behave and how you treat others. That's more than half the battle of getting diversity "right" in the workplace. At the very least, you'll come a long way from doing it wrong.

This reminds me of the analogy we've all heard about how a brilliant idea is symbolized by a light bulb going off over your head. Well, I don't know about most folks, but in my house, when I'm dealing with the dark because of a burnt-out bulb, a new light doesn't just appear. Getting a new light bulb requires me to visit the storage cabinet, and if the right kind of bulb isn't there, then I need to drive to the closest open store. Then I have to come back home and fiddle around in the dark to find the socket to screw in the new bulb. In other words, enlightenment requires effort. It doesn't just happen.

And that's what thinking differently about diversity requires—effort. Not necessarily work or strain, not always discomfort, but good old-fashioned effort.

Anyway, you have probably figured it out already, but the title of this book—*The Diversity Code*—is a twist on the title of the best-selling novel by Dan Brown, *The Da Vinci Code*. I got very excited when I came up with the title because for most of us, trying to figure out diversity in the workplace feels like trying to break a big encrypted code where someone—we never know who—is the keeper of the big book that holds the key to figuring out all the mysteries and puzzles that getting a good grasp on diversity requires. This book will help you move toward solving those mysteries and puzzles.

Oftentimes while reading this book, you'll understand the spirit of a quote by Walt Whitman that I love: "Do I contradict myself? Very well, then I contradict myself." Authentic and practical diversity is not about rules and regulations that put you in compliance. You can legally comply with the law but still be really, really lousy at promoting diversity in your workplace, whether you are a manager or a regular employee.

## Divas and Diversity

I became a "diva" after I dubbed myself so (and also because the word *diva* and the word *diversity* begin with the same three letters).

It may sound a bit corny, but I've had to deal with diversity my whole life—even when there wasn't a name for it, let alone practically a social and educational movement about it. My first diversity lesson came when I was a little black kid going to a predominantly white Catholic school, when my family lived in the "hood" and thought a rosary was a place where you kept flowers. Since then, I've negotiated multiple worlds a multitude of times in my life. Throughout, I have managed to use the skill of being myself while trying to understand everyone else around me. Sometimes, that's all real-life diversity is—being yourself while allowing others to be themselves, too.

For several years, I practiced employment law as an attorney, primarily working for prominent law firms in Kansas City, Missouri. I represented some major national and local companies that got slapped with discrimination lawsuits and employee complaints. The thing that was particularly interesting about having that role is that I'm a black woman. It's interesting because when I would show up for depositions, people would often get confused and think I was the plaintiff, the court reporter, a witness, maybe the plaintiff's attorney, and sometimes—even if I was wearing a suit—a delivery person showing up in the wrong conference room. Usually, no one expected the part of the attorney for the "da Man" to be played by an African-American woman. And let's not talk about how much more people got surprised and confused after I began wearing my hair in dreadlocks.

Long before I became an attorney, I was a journalist and a writer, and when the opportunity to write the book that became *Working While Black* came along, I was in heaven. I had found someone to pay me to do the two things I most liked to do—write and educate others on issues regarding diversity.

I continued to work as an attorney but felt disenchanted with the law. Once I started getting an increasing number of chances to write and speak about diversity, I found myself becoming even more disenchanted with the practice of law. Employment law is oftentimes about trying to resolve a problem and fix blame long after the problem is over rather than trying to anticipate and avoid the issue before it begins. Even in employment law, the stereotypical image of the ambulance chaser isn't too far off—one where too many lawyers get caught up in assigning blame and fighting about liability. After a while, I just got to the point where all I cared about was figuring out how someone could have stopped the metaphorical car accident in the first place.

As part of my journey on the road to diversity, I realized that average people don't have a natural tendency to put themselves in the shoes of other people or even at the very least attempt to understand why other people are wearing moccasins or Prada pumps in the first place. So, I observed that a lot of clashing took place because the world was getting more complex and diverse, but no one—and I mean no one, not just whites or men—was bothering to learn new ways of looking at situations.

And as my eyes begin to see differently, I seemed to attract more kinds of opportunities and work experiences that led me to becoming an expert on diversity. One of those opportunities was the column "Dear Diversity Diva" that I proposed to the *Kansas City Star*. The column has run in the newspaper's Business section since January 2008. It's a question–and–answer column where anyone can write in a question about how to handle a specific issue or problem in the workplace involving diversity.

## A Book for Everyone

All of my experiences dealing with the various facets of employment and diversity led me to want to write a book that anyone could read and benefit from—leaders as well as regular working stiffs, people with numbers and privilege on their side as well as people feeling pummeled by their minority status. I particularly wanted this to be a book that managers and other workplace leaders could use as a tool to help them to attract the best people to their workforce and to extract the best from the people they find.

Each chapter in this book is divided into three parts. Each chapter title is posed as a question, and the beginning of each chapter is a letter posing the same question, similar to the letters readers send me in my "Dear Diversity Diva" column.

The second part of each chapter is where I answer the question and really expound on it. I expound on it in a way that blends my experience as a diversity consultant, my knowledge as an employment attorney, and my philosophy as an individual living and working with diversity issues.

The third part of each chapter gives a diversity exercise that you "take on the road" as if this were a week-long diversity workshop where you apply what you are submerging yourself in—a diversity boot camp, so to speak.

But I understand that, like me, a lot of people hate exercises at the end of chapters. They feel too much like they're being treated as a slow student who has just been lectured and now needs simple homework to reinforce the lessons. That's why I like to think of my exercises as more like a Sudoku puzzle or a crossword puzzle, where the exercises are designed more to show off how smart you are and to address that human instinct to want to investigate and figure out the mysteries and puzzles of diversity for yourself.

I wasn't even trying to be clever and tie the exercises and puzzles back to the fact that the book is called *The Diversity Code,* but the connection works for me if it does for you. I could have taken the route of getting all cutesy and invented some code schematic in trying to "decipher" diversity in the workplace, something that would be fun and clever and might even get me booked on the *Today* show. But it wouldn't necessarily make you think or look at things in a slightly different way. The exercises at the end of the chapter are as cute as I get, and my hope is that they are actually helpful.

Please note that throughout this book, I make occasional references to political, social, and even pop culture examples that may appear to have absolutely nothing to do with workplace diversity. But they do. Because when it comes to diversity—the way people see, hear, reason through, and live with and through the differences of others—there is no out of bounds.

## The End of the Day

At the end of the day, with true diversity, the code is getting in the habit of recognizing the differences in others, being able to manage those differences, and feeling comfortable in doing so. The code breaker is each individual's internal motivation to do so.

While diversity and inclusion issues are responsibilities that every employee has to some extent, the responsibilities are particularly in the hands of those who manage the workplace. These people must have more than an adequate grasp on the subject. Managers and workplace leaders—which includes HR employees—can't afford to be myopic when it comes to the employees they lead if they want to stay on top of managing a diverse workforce and making sure that even when the numbers look good, people are actually working in a way that encourages diversity.

"He who can no longer pause to wonder and stand rapt in awe,
is as good as dead; his eyes are closed."
—Albert Einstein

# CHAPTER ONE

# How Do You Define Diversity?

*Dear Diversity Diva:*

*Is diversity a fancy way of saying that we all have to drink the Kool-Aid and indulge in being all P.C. so we don't hurt anyone's feelings and worry about getting sued or fired or both?*

*Signed,*
*P.O.'ed About Having to Be P.C.*

## Deciding on a Definition

Not to get all Bill Clinton, but I feel the pain of anyone who thinks diversity is a synonym for political correctness. Diversity can be confusing, it can be irritating, and it can just straight up be a pain in the butt. But it's not just about being politically correct, or P.C.

Talking about diversity can definitely be circular, where it's hard to determine which should come first—caring about diversity and then working to figure it out, or working to figure it out so that you care. It's just like the chicken and the egg. Which comes first? The chicken that has to lay the egg or the egg that creates a new chicken? Ultimately, though, does it matter which comes first?

I do know this and so do you: It is confusing to know what is current and "correct" with every group of individuals who bond over an identity and with every issue that attracts a group of individuals. Is it black or African-American? Is it disabled or handicapped? Is it Hispanic if I know that someone is a Mexican-American? What's the difference between gay, lesbian, bisexual, and transgender? And why can I call a rug Oriental but not a person? Hey, even for those of us who deal with it all the time, it can be confusing!

What is the real issue here? Does it matter knowing why diversity is important, or is it more crucial to know what diversity is?

For me, diversity starts with a definition, because if you do not like how I define it, you will not bother to decide whether the topic is important anyway.

## My Definition of Diversity

My personal definition—after years of talking about it, writing about it, litigating it, mediating it, and just thinking about it whenever I so much as watch a television commercial—is the following: *Diversity is seeing the differences, distinctions, and dividing lines of others with a soft gaze but with clear vision.*

That's my personal definition, which I think works as a great starting point for what diversity is and what diversity is not.

When I say "seeing the differences," I mean the obvious, usually immutable ones—differences of race, color, gender, national origin, sexual orientation, and physical abilities.

When I say seeing "distinctions," I'm talking about the distinctions between the differences. I'm talking about understanding that an East Coast lesbian who is black with a Jewish mother might be having a different life experience than a married black woman who is Southern born and raised. To the naked eye, you may just see two black women, but by seeing their distinctions, you see that they very well could be worlds apart in the key ways they look at the world and operate in the workplace.

When I say seeing "dividing lines," I'm talking about the life choices that define how people live their lives—the dividing lines where people decide on their political parties, their leanings within the parties, their positions based on religion and family upbringing, and sometimes even whether you swear by bottled water versus tap.

## Seeing Without Judgment

When I say in my definition of diversity that one should see "with a soft gaze but with clear vision," it's a fancier way of saying that we should see others without judgment.

Actually, in all fairness, when I say "without judgment" what I really mean is with an awareness of the fact that you are judging and questioning yourself as to whether judgment in a particular situation is relevant, let alone fair. We all judge, whether we want to admit it or not. With workplace diversity, however, it's a matter of whether judging serves any legitimate purpose.

Let's say you see an apple in a fruit bowl. Depending on where you are, you first decide if it's a real apple or one of those tricky decorations that's so realistic looking you might accidentally bite into it. You decide it's an apple—a *real* apple, not a fake apple. And you decide it's an apple—as opposed to an orange or a banana or a potato or a tomato—before you get to anything else. You don't have any angry attachments or sad feelings about deciding whether it's an apple.

Now, if you're hungry and you don't like apples, you might be irritated that the bowl holds apples instead of fruit that you do like, but that thought comes after you look at the object and decide that it's an apple. A picky person might argue that you're "judging" apples if you're irritated that the bowl holds apples instead of kiwi. But if the point is deciding whether you want to eat what's in the bowl, then the judging holds a legitimate purpose if you don't want to eat apples.

When it comes to people, it appears that as a society we increasingly rely more on judging others. This is because the more we encourage and encounter differences in our society, the more we have to make ourselves feel safer by judging what we think others are about.

So while seeing with a soft gaze but with clear vision is easier to do with a bowl of fruit, it's far more important to do with the people you work with and manage.

## The Heart of the Matter

At its heart, diversity is *not* about what you say or what you do. It is about how you think. And how you think is what determines what you say or do. The diversity code presented in this book is about giving you mental tools to change your thinking about diversity so that you have a better chance of creating, working in, and managing workplaces that succeed. In other words, workplaces where people are not constantly engaging in battles of perspective, viewpoint, and will based on ego that end up turning into complaints, lawsuits, and generally unproductive environments where there is more frustration and resentment than cooperation.

Most people hate thinking about diversity when they feel the topic is forced upon them. When it comes to diversity in the workplace, just put out a memo announcing a mandatory diversity seminar, workshop, or training session and see how loud the groans get. Sure, there are a few people who look forward to a diversity get-together either because they think it's an easy way to get out of work for a few hours or they genuinely believe that the meeting will get to the heart of whatever diversity issues they have observed. These people are the minority, though.

One of the reasons why diversity can be a touchy if not downright divisive topic is that it is all about your perspective, and what often happens with perspective is that most people don't see any other way of looking at a situation other than through their own eyes. Therefore, when someone has a different perspective, the presumption is that the other person or group is being deliberately contrary or willfully insensitive.

The great modern-day philosopher Woody Allen once said, "The lion and the calf shall lie down together but the calf won't get much sleep." Where diversity can get weedy is that people are often surprised by which people view themselves as lions and which view themselves as calves. Groups with more power, for example, often express that they feel "held hostage" by the concerns of various minority or special interest groups— as if they will always be held in the wrong no matter what because of their historic power and larger numbers. That's why part of what *The Diversity Code* aims to teach is how to talk to people so that you can figure out where they are really coming from and not just where you presume they are coming from.

## Opposites Can Distract

Another way of looking at how to define diversity is by looking at it through its opposite impression. The opposite of diversity is not sameness, blandness, or monotony, the way most people think it is. But those descriptions are close. Instead, the opposite of diversity is *norm* or *baseline*. Basically, when people think about whether a workplace is diverse, they have in their heads a subtle, hazy thought of what they expect a place to look like, and then anybody added in who is different is considered to have made the place diverse.

Take, for example, going to the hospital to see a doctor. Assume that the hospital is in a "good" neighborhood, the doctor has been recommended by friends or an insurance company, and you have zero prior knowledge of the hospital. Usually, at the back of your mind (unless it's an OB-GYN), you expect the doctor to be a white male. Why? Because despite the recent advent of shows like *Grey's Anatomy* (which features doctors who are not white, not male, and sometimes not either), that's what we've been socialized to expect from being reared on everything from television shows to movies to most people's life experiences. (As an example of how deep that expectation can manifest itself, a colleague of mine said that when she put herself through school and worked at a hospital reception desk, she was surprised at the number of people who specifically requested that they did not want a doctor who was a member of racial minority group. The reason voiced by the people who gave a reason was the assumption that white doctors were better.)

When you have a child and take him to a new grade school and meet the first-grade teacher, you expect the teacher to be female. Why? Because that's what we've been socialized on. My point isn't about racism or sexism. It's about expectations of what we think the norm is.

If you go to an Indian restaurant, love the food, ask to meet the chef, and find out it's a seventy-two-year-old Puerto Rican woman, you're going to be surprised. That's not what you expected. It's not what you expect to be the "norm" for people cooking in an Indian restaurant.

Ironically, the more varied and different our society gets, the more we rely on the mental norms in our head to allow us to bounce gracefully from one situation to the next. But in the workplace, having expectations of what the norm should be gets you into real trouble because, theoretically, the doors of employment are open to everyone.

I've always described the U.S. workplace as a busy intersection rather than a melting pot. If you can't stand those "damn gays," guess whom you're going to have to deal with as your next department head? A "damn gay." If you don't quite trust anyone from an Arab country, you're going to have quite the dilemma when you enter a new position and discover that a very Arab-looking person is your administrative assistant, and your employer makes it clear that no change is allowed.

You can pick the people you date, the people you may eventually marry, your neighborhoods, your friends, your places of worship, and your social clubs, but just like with family, you can't pick who will compose the landscape of your work day. At least with family, you can avoid certain people until you have to attend funerals, weddings, and reunions. But with the workplace, you have to learn to work it out for about forty hours a week.

Especially in certain parts of the country where people are more limited in how they view diversity, white guys can sometimes be heard to say, "But I don't have diversity, I'm just a white guy." First of all, that assumption is false because the underlying implication is that white males are the norm, and thus they can never be the ones providing diversity to a situation. Second, another key reason why the analysis falls short is that the implication is that their race and their gender are the only identifications that define them.

## Everyone Has a Story

I inherited my grandmother's gift (and sometimes curse) of having perfect strangers tell me their life story within about thirty seconds of meeting me.

As a newspaper reporter, an employment litigation attorney, and a diversity consultant and writer, this has certainly come in handy over the years.

One Christmas Day, I was sitting next to a woman in a restaurant as we waited for our respective relatives to meet us. She and I struck up a conversation. I could tell from the context of the conversation that she was about my mother's age, but while my mother looks years younger than her chronological age, the woman looked years older.

In our short time together, I learned that she had two kids—a daughter who died at age 40 from lupus after a long bout with cancer that she had beaten, and a grown son she and her husband weren't speaking to, and thus were not spending Christmas with because of an ugly fight with their daughter-in-law.

This woman was a different race from me, was from a different generation, and clearly had a host of life experiences I have never had and would never have. She was very sweet despite her sadness mixed with a tinge of anger, and the last thing she said to me was, "Thanks for letting me dump on you. I know everyone has a story."

As I thought about that brief encounter and what the woman had said, it hit me that "everyone has a story" is the seed of what diversity really is about. You can't know everybody's story in the workplace, and oftentimes it's not even appropriate to know. But understanding and accepting differences is about having compassion for the humanity of the people you work with that seeps through even the smallest interaction.

Too often, people feel they have to "approve" of a difference before they can treat it as important. And that's not what diversity is truly all about. By "approve," I mean that most people feel as if they have to understand a difference or at least value the difference before they are willing to accept it as a valid difference. A big example of this is physical disability: If you can see that a person walks slowly with a cane, then it's infinitely easier to accept that she can't walk as quickly with you to an impromptu meeting as someone who doesn't walk with a cane. You can accept the physical limitation because it's visible, it's understandable, it's beyond the person's control, and it probably doesn't conflict with any existing value you have.

But many differences aren't that cut-and-dried, and thus, the issue of approval comes in. Let's say you're dealing with someone who speaks with an accent because he is a first-generation American whose parents are from another country. This difference may be obvious, understandable, and beyond the person's control. But some people have strong opinions about immigration laws, assumptions about people being illegal immigrants, and irritation that members of particular groups are competing with members of their particular group for opportunities in the workplace. Thus, some people won't approve of this difference.

A less essential example is how one views animals. It makes no difference whether you agree that or approve of how a dog is not a cat—but failure to understand that a difference exists and acknowledging how that difference manifests is the difference between having a healthy, thriving, loving pet or not. Some people don't like dogs, some don't like cats, but there is rarely any conflict of values associated with identifying whether an animal is a dog or a cat.

Most people don't come to work and put on their "working" hat, which excludes all their references points. Instead, when individuals are at work, they come in wearing their "people" hat, and it's one they can never take off. They can't take off the clothing of their upbringing, their various group memberships, the individual experiences they've lived through, and certainly not the last thing they may have heard on the car radio or their cell phone podcast before they entered their work space.

All of these experiences are an influence, and influences affect the effects of diversity in the workplace.

## The Power of Opinions

In trying to break the code of diversity in the workplace in any meaningful way, one must remember the power and the impact of opinions. Everyone has them about every little thing.

In the workplace, opinions can be a dangerous thing when it comes to diversity because oftentimes the opinions are about people. Worse, about categories of people. Opinions can be completely insidious and damaging because facts falter in the face of strong opinions. People hold on to their opinions with the fierceness of a parent holding on to the hand of a toddler in a moving crowd.

There are a number of ways that people attempt to discount, dismiss, or dismantle the opinions of others that they don't like.

## Questioning to Dismantle, Not to Understand

People can question the motivation of the person with the opinion. This can happen even when the person is reciting what she has actually observed. People who do not like the observations may convert what is witnessed to an opinion that is tainted by some "bad" motivation of the witness reciting the observations.

I recently talked to an investigator of employment matters. She complained about the tendency of company representatives to rush and tell her whether someone had been on probation or passed over for a promotion right before she is scheduled to talk to the person about what he saw or heard in a harassment investigation. Even though she repeatedly tells the representatives that the person's status is irrelevant to what he observed, it seems completely relevant to the company representatives, who want the negative statement of the employee to be discounted.

Ironically, in one particular case, the investigator found that it was the company representative's motivation that was suspect. The representative kept telling her information that she specifically said she didn't want to hear about the employees she was going to interview in an investigation he held a strong opinion about. This is a valid concern because it is necessary to interview witnesses to gather facts in employment matters, and part of gathering facts is obtaining them first and then evaluating the weight, validity, and reasonableness of those facts.

Out of the employment context, for example, if the only witness to a car accident is a man walking his dog, and I'm an investigator, I have to ask the man what he saw and get that down. In the course of my investigation, if I smell alcohol on the man's breath or find out that one of the people in the car is the man that his ex-wife left him for, those issues will impact the weight I give to what he saw. *But* as the investigator I am still required to get the information, since tainted motivations do not necessarily lead to tainted observations. Or, to put it another way, everyone's motivations are tainted by something, even if it's just being distracted by what's playing on the radio, so it's always a matter of separating taint from truth.

## Undermining Methodology

Another method used to discount an opinion you don't like is to write off the methodology of what the opinion is based on. You could write it off because it's based on personal experience, because "I've never read that anywhere before," or because the person who said it doesn't have a degree or has too many degrees. While it's understandable and the smart thing to do to find out how people have acquired the factual information they are trying to impart as knowledge or information, you have to remember that opinions are different.

For example, if a person makes a statement about a political subject and uses specific statistics from a study mentioned in the newspaper that morning, the response of "I don't believe anything published by that liberal rag" is discounting the methodology. That's particularly so if the person can cite several different places where the same statistics were reported. Now if the opinion is based on what a columnist—who is paid to write with a slant—says, then it's not discounting the methodology to disagree with the opinion of the columnist.

## *Fighting an Opinion with an Opinion*

That ties in to another way that people dismiss opinions that they don't like—by using their own experiences and opinions to cancel out the opinions of another person. This comes up quite frequently when someone has a cultural bias about a segment of society that contradicts someone else's cultural bias.

Another way to dismiss another person's opinion is to counter it with another opinion and call that second opinion fact. Anyone who has ever listened to political talk radio on either end of the political spectrum knows that talk show hosts have that technique down to a science.

## *Turning an Opinion into One Other Than That Being Expressed*

Taking an opinion and twisting it into something that was not actually said is another classic approach of dismantling an opinion. This method is particularly effective when you are passing the opinion on to others outside the hearing of the original speaker and where that person doesn't have a chance to correct the interpretation layered on top of what was really said.

For example, Molly tells Frederica that she is against their company offering benefits for domestic partners. Molly explains carefully that her point is that the benefit extends to heterosexuals, and that's not fair to her as a single person because heterosexuals have the option of getting legally married. Well, if all Frederica passes on is that Molly is against domestic partnership benefits, without the underlying reason of why, she's taken Molly's sensitive opinion out of context and created a whole new opinion, which might make people think Molly is homophobic.

All these approaches to dealing with the opinions of others that you don't like can be a huge impediment to any advances or breakthroughs on diversity in your particular workplace, which is why examining how and why your workers express and react to opinions is a key task for anyone managing diversity in the workplace.

## Keys to Breaking This Chapter's Code

- It's okay to accept that diversity can be difficult, uncomfortable, hard to follow, and sometimes a downright pain in the butt.

- Diversity is the habit of seeing the differences, distinctions, and dividing lines of others with a soft gaze but with a clear vision.

- Everyone has his or her own story, and everyone else has an opinion about someone else's story—even when we don't think that we do.

## Diversity Exercise

This very first exercise is a variation on an ice-breaking exercise done in some diversity seminars. Mine, however, doesn't require you to actually go up and ask people questions directly, which could be a bit embarrassing.

For the next day or two, when you're in a public place where you can observe a lot of people at once—the grocery store, the gas station, a concert, a party with a lot of strangers—see if you can determine if anybody you see is in one of the following categories:

- Has been married more than three times

- Has a GED and also holds at least one college degree

- Has danced at a honky-tonk bar

- Sports more than four tattoos on his or her body

- Grew up with at least six siblings

- Has read all seven Harry Potter books

- Has a child by someone of another race

- Proclaims a different sexual orientation today than when he or she was twenty-one years old

It's funny how difficult it is to figure out these things from just looking at people, yet we do this in reverse all the time—making up stories about who we think people are based on what they look like, what they wear, how they move, etc.

## Group Exercise

This can also be converted into a group exercise that managers can have a team of employees do. Print out enough copies of the above list to pass around, and then have the employees go around the room to initial the items on the list that they can say yes to.

This will prompt a good conversation afterward about the difficulty of how you have to make a lot of assumptions about people to do this exercise and the awkwardness of walking up to someone with that assumption.

# CHAPTER TWO

# Can You Tell Me What Diversity Isn't?

*Dear Diversity Diva:*

*Tell it like it is instead of using all this hippie, feel good, P.C. stuff called diversity. Pure and simple, diversity is about quotas and hiring goals, isn't it?*

*Signed,*
*Quoting Quotas and Galled About Goals*

## Diversity Is Not Just About Numbers

One of the biggest fallacies about diversity is that it's all about the numbers. After all, if you have enough discernible difference in a room, then you have diversity, right? If, for example, there is a work meeting where there are twenty-one executives, and one executive is Hispanic and two are female, is the meeting diverse? Does your answer change if the company has its headquarters in San Antonio, Texas, or if the company is a cosmetics corporation? Does your answer depend on whether any of the executives have any visible physical disabilities and the company manufactures wheelchairs?

Say the company is a generic business whose mission serves a wide, across-the-board spectrum of humanity, such as making toilet paper or simple ink pens—something that everyone uses. Then what do the numbers reveal? Does this change your answer? More important, who determines diversity—the person from the group most comfortably represented, or the odd man or woman out?

The lack of diversity, or difference, can be determined by the naked eye if you are judging the diversity of the room only on the basis of race, gender, age, or obvious physical disability. Pretty much everything else takes an extra set of questions or more extensive observation.

Take sexual orientation, for example. Contrary to what some people think, sexual orientation isn't something that can necessarily be determined by how people walk, hold a glass, wear their hair, or any of the other stereotypical ways people think they are determining sexuality. Even when people act or move in stereotypical ways when in private social settings, they may act totally different in the workplace, where people consciously and subconsciously conform their behavior and mannerisms to fit in. The same thing can happen with some ethnic groups. The word choice, syntax, and information presented can dramatically change in private.

How does this play out in the workplace? The answer is that if people can't determine who is "different" from obvious visual cues, then it is very easy to assume that homogeneity rather than diversity is at play, even when the opposite is true. When that is the case, people can engage in behavior and assumptions that can be offensive to others or create an environment where some individuals are distinctly uncomfortable.

## Diversity Isn't Just the Perspective of the Person Providing It: What Is the Norm?

Often in the workplace, people like to act as if the difference of one or two individuals lets the whole department or company off the hook because that person or persons have provided the diversity. At diversity workshops, for example, white men love to joke about how "they have no diversity." In part, that joke comes from assessing diversity based on what can best be seen with open eyes: race and gender. But in part (and it's the part that makes the whole topic trickier), it's because by being white males, they think they are setting the "norm" and thus aren't providing any diversity to the group assembled.

Granted, there are some white men who tell this joke because they are feeling nervous discomfort. But there are also a lot of white men who genuinely feel they have no diversity, and the men who feel that way are often the ones who have the most resentment about having to attend anything associated with diversity. Managers and HR people who hear those comments need to probe deeper to see where people are coming from—if, for example, they are coming from a place of awkward self-consciousness or if they are coming from a place of resentment.

Everyone provides diversity to the equation. Everyone. People aren't interchangeable. Neither are their backgrounds, credentials, histories, accomplishments, or other ways that they stray from everyone else in the room. While individuals in a work situation are replaceable, they are never interchangeable.

Even if you break it down by demographics rather than individual experiences, no two white men share the same makeup. At some point, religion or spiritual worldview, age, regional upbringing, social-economic upbringing, sexual orientation and experiences, marital status, familial status, physical abilities and disabilities, education, and hobbies cause some divergence in perspective. In the workplace, that divergence of perspective might cause one man to have an approach to a problem that is radically different from that of the other man.

Therefore, it is misleading to look to the person who is visibly "different" as the person providing all the diversity in the room. It's misleading because often the diversity judged is only skin deep. And it's misleading because it perpetuates the fallacy that there is a norm and those falling outside the norm aren't "normal."

As I explain later in the book, the government has legal reporting requirements regarding race and gender. And race and gender are often the first and easiest ways we self-identify as children and then identify others once we move outside the playpen. However, diversity as a practical matter is far more expansive than that.

That's why the concept of "norm" goes way beyond race and gender. For example, in any public meeting in the United States, with the exception of meetings regarding certain narrow and specific issues, the assumption is that everyone in the room is heterosexual. The language used is usually the first sign that everything flows from that presumption. This is especially true if the topic of conversation has anything to do with families, since as a society, unless the work environment is particularly progressive, people don't necessarily associate gay with children.

Even in workplace situations where the topics at meetings are less personal, if there is any need to refer to husbands, wives, or spouses, the concept of "life partners" is rarely included. Why? Because the norm is being straight, and those outside the norm aren't deliberately excluded as much as just not thought of in the first place.

Religion is another place where certain norms are assumed, even in the workplace. Even in the most casual references, people make allusions that assume that everyone in the room is Christian or comes from a Christian background. An example is the use of the term "Christmas party" in most U.S. companies. Sure, most companies may formally refer to their winter festivity as a "holiday party," but almost all informal conversation makes mention of Christmas parties. If a Fortune 500 company suddenly started calling its annual December party a "Hanukkah party," there would be a distinct and most likely audible reaction from the workforce. Why? Because despite the frequent reference to our being a Judeo-Christian–based society, the distinct emphasis is on the Christian part, and therefore Jewish religious references are considered outside the norm.

## Diversity Is Not Political Correctness

Imagine that you had a new coworker named William. When you met him, you said, "Nice to meet you, Billy. You don't mind if I call you Billy, do you?" If he told you he would prefer to be called William, then you probably would immediately stop calling him Billy.

You probably wouldn't feel any emotion or deep-seated resentfulness. You certainly wouldn't denigrate William or argue with him. You would recognize your misstep—really, your presumption of familiarity—and keep right on moving. His correction probably wouldn't create a crack in your work relationship. The one thing you almost definitely would not do is reduce William's request to be called by the name he chooses to political correctness or being P.C.

Unfortunately, when it comes to how groups (other than the ones that you belong to) like to be referred to, talked about, or perceived, it's easy to blow off their preferences. It's easy to say that groups are being overly sensitive or unnecessarily difficult or that you need to be politically correct.

Irritation can spring from the fact that people don't understand why another group has a preference that varies from what they are used to doing. For example, the switch from colored to Negro to Afro-American to black to African-American has confused many a person. Yet other people have adjusted seamlessly to the transition, understanding or at least respecting the historical and societal implications that each change has.

Many people also recognize that what is preferable to one individual may be different for another. (I, for example, am a black person who is not a big fan of the term "African-American" because it's inaccurate in that not all blacks are African descendants. Meanwhile, my grandmother, who is from an entirely different generation, had an almost visceral disdain for the term "black" because black was a distinctly negative term in the time and place where she grew up.) But if you're the kind of person who is more comfortable with fixed, logical, linear decisions and perceptions that change at the rate rock forms, you will find every societal shift aggravating and an irritating example of political correctness gone haywire.

The solution—if there is one—for this dilemma is to ask questions. Ask people their preferences in cases where you don't know. Research online or in books to develop a fuller understanding of what you fail to understand. When you do that, it becomes less about P.C. than about just being considerate of others.

And if you don't want to go to the extra work of educating yourself when it comes to being generally informed, at a minimum stay current with the preferences of the coworkers you interact with.

## The Role of Stereotypes in Diversity

In any diversity workshop, you can hear stereotypes trumpeted as the absolutely worst thing to rely on when dealing with other people. They are the Kryptonite of diversity. But when it comes to getting gritty and raw about the underpinnings of what diversity is not, you have to start with stereotypes.

Stereotypes are usually so ingrained in everyone's thinking that most are no more questioned than the way drivers would question why their feet automatically tap the brake when the light is about to turn red at an intersection. People who at least know they were brought up on stereotypes or who realize that they harbor them now have a much shorter road to travel than the people who believe that they have valid opinions of others based on what they think are facts. The stereotypes that get us in trouble are the ones that we let guide us and that give us the illusion that we're merely observing patterns rather than relying on stereotypes.

Stereotypes aren't always about other groups. People can also have distinct negative biases (one definition for stereotypes) about the very group they belong to.

What is troubling about stereotypes is that there can be a thin line between negative assessments based on groups and how they affect your opinion of the real live person in front of you who is a member of that group.

For example, studies have shown that height makes a difference in the workplace that translates to dollars and cents (if not common sense). After researchers made corrections for variables regarding weight, gender, and age, the studies found that an inch of height is worth $789 a year in salary.[1] Considering the biases that people have about height—particularly in regard to men—it's not a reach to think how differently people perceive the competencies of a tall man standing in front of them compared to the competencies of a shorter one. Worse, these prejudices also factor in when the bias isn't remotely conscious or deliberate.

Even when one is managing "up"—in other words, being conscious of how you treat the people who supervise you—the reliance on stereotype instead of assessment of the individual can cause you to perceive your male boss as arrogant or your female boss as "bitchy" before he or she has done one thing to earn that label. Once you've gone to that place in your mind, anything they do that supports the stereotype reinforces the foundation of "facts" you rely on to continue sustaining the stereotype.

## The Road Between Individual Assessment and Overreaching Stereotype

Isn't there someplace between applying stereotypes and making individual assessments about every person you work with where patterns can be made, conclusions drawn, and assumptions safely drawn? Sure. There always is because as thinking, sentient beings with the power to create the experiences we live, we can always choose to observe and use the observations as context to help figure out individuals. And in time, if the observations and conclusions you jump to get challenged or contradicted enough, then your observations shape into different conclusions.

The best and most fair way to form and change your conclusions and observations as necessary is to keep your eyes open so that you're constantly and comprehensively observing and testing the surrounding and supporting assessments you come to. People have a bad habit of seeing only what they want to see and only what supports their worldview.

One observation I've made in the workplace that borders on being a stereotype (and I couldn't argue if I was accused of this being a full-blown stereotype) is what I've called PAWW activity. PAWW stands for Passive Aggressive Working Woman. It refers to the observation that a large number of workplace issues involving women arise from a segment of women who have not learned how to deal directly and effectively with others.

Now, one can argue that this is a stereotype because I'm casting an aspersion on a group of people. If I left it at all women or all white women or all women in positions of authority, then it would clearly be a stereotype. Also, if I assume that a woman I meet is a PAWW before I know anything about her, then I'm acting on a stereotype even if it is not a blanket one.

Basically, the concept of PAWW gives me a framework for choosing how I deal with an individual who fits into a pattern I've seen over and over again. My use of this as a paradigm is informal and personal. But anyone who has worked in corporate America long enough has probably participated in formal patterns of identifying and classifying work, communication, and leadership styles. For example, the Myers-Briggs Type Indicator® assessment is a popular personality test given in the workplace to determine which of sixteen personality types a person is, based on the answers to specific questions. Sure, people may find that more palatable than my PAWW observations, because the Myers-Briggs is a methodology approved by the field of psychology, but it still breaks down to patterns about people that could be abused as a stereotype.

The biggest problem with stereotypes is that they are often unconscious, and we operate on them without realizing that we are. People can have a clear, firm understanding and perception of their own bias against a particular group of people and even internally check themselves regarding that bias when they meet someone new from that group. But what about the hundreds, if not thousands, of mental thoughts that people have each day that still use that bias as its backdrop?

For example, let's say Manuel has a bias against overweight people. He knows he has this bias. He even feels a little bit bad about having it. He does his best to not let it interfere with his hiring practices or the people he decides to promote. Nevertheless, the bias exists. What if Manuel has a tendency to judge Nancy—who is overweight—harder in the section of the annual employee evaluation that deals with initiative because she doesn't move with the same level of "go get 'em energy" as Paul, who is lanky and energetic? Isn't there a chance that Manuel's bias against overweight people has crept into his workplace judgment despite his best efforts to beat it down?

There's always that possibility, which is why awareness of why and how you come to decisions is a key part of unraveling how you weave diversity into your daily work. That awareness is a way of thinking about diversity that should be in place as long as you have to work with others.

## Keys to Breaking This Chapter's Code

- Diversity is not just about numbers and it's never about quotas from a legal standpoint, even though people tend to make this link in their minds.

- A discernable difference—such as race and gender—isn't the only deciding factor in determining diversity.

- Stereotypes can act as a guidepost to help you keep your bearings, but asking questions keeps you from being mired in stereotypes and helps you know when to throw them away.

## Diversity Exercise

For one day, (or for at least two or three set hours if you can't stand a whole day or it isn't practical), ask yourself internally if every statement coming out of the mouths of people you talk to is an opinion or a fact. The trick to this exercise is that you do this for every statement you hear, not just the important ones or interesting ones or ones that you think relate directly to diversity. You must apply it to everything that you hear people say.

For example, if someone says, "The weather is awful today," ask yourself if that person's statement is a statement of fact or an opinion about a fact. Do this even if it is raining so much that there was visibility of only two feet when you drove to work this morning. In this example, some may say that it's practically a fact that the day is awful when it's pouring so hard—but it's not an awful day to a man who wants his garden to grow, a woman who wants to avoid a school field trip with her children, a college student looking for an excuse to sleep in, or anyone relieved to see the rain after weeks of temperatures in the 100s.

Let's take the example to a more work-related comment. Your supervisor says that she needs to put a note in a subordinate's file because the employee has been late too many times. Now, you have seen that employee come in past his starting time more than once, so to you it's a fact. But probe deeper (not verbally to your supervisor unless in some way it's part of your job description to have that discussion) to see if it's a fact that the employee has been late "too many times." Ask yourself if you have noticed any other employees who have also been late or if the supervisor has identified specific rules regarding tardiness that this particular employee would have violated.

Make it a game. Keep asking yourself questions about a statement. Strip the statement to its essence.

Opinion? Fact? Opinionated Fact? Factual Opinion? You be the judge.

If you do this exercise for even a couple of hours, you will be shocked by how many people—yourself included—operate on facts that aren't really facts.

## Group Exercise

Have every person in the room give a five-word or five-phrase description of how he or she would describe themselves. If people ask if it should be a physical description, tell them that it is up to them. Have people share their lists, and notice any themes. For example, see if the people who stand out in any way tend to have that more in their description than others. Examine the different ways that people choose to self-identify, noting that some people focus on the physical, others on personality, and still others on the roles they play in their lives. Talk about how the way they self-identify can impact their work experience in a way that is different from how others choose to identify them.

## Note

1.   Timothy A. Judge and Daniel M. Cable, "The Effect of Physical Height on Workplace Success and Income: Preliminary Test of a Theoretical Model," *Journal of Applied Psychology* 89, no. 3 (June 2004): 428–441.

# CHAPTER THREE

# What Is the Basic Law
# on Discrimination?

*Dear Diversity Diva:*

*I understand that diversity is supposed to be about getting along with different kinds of folks, and I've been to all these harassment and diversity workshops that my job makes me go to. But tell the truth: Isn't diversity just another way of saying we should stop doing things that might get our company hit with a lawsuit?*

*Signed,*
*Dealing Out the Real Deal*

## The Truth About Avoiding Lawsuits

One of the facts about diversity as a workplace issue is that there are as many reasons that people find diversity important as there are people who actually find the subject of diversity important. And yes, the truth is that one of the reasons that many leaders of businesses and organizations find diversity and inclusion a critical issue is because a workplace that makes diversity a low priority leaves itself far more open to allegations of discrimination. Allegations sometimes lead to actual legal complaints, and lawsuits can be costly to companies in terms of both money and productivity.

Some argue that the media exaggerates the frequency and size of discrimination lawsuits in the workplace, giving the impression that every other employee with a gripe brings a complaint. But the fact is that even if just a few employees in a multimillion- or billion-dollar operation accuse a company of discrimination or some other unlawful job-related offense, it triggers a team of high-powered and high-priced defense attorneys, which cuts a lot more into a company's bottom line than a business wants. And that doesn't include the residual effect of bad publicity if the complaints go public.

## So What Is Discrimination Really?

If you'd like a dictionary explanation of the noun *discrimination,* one dictionary gives the following as one definition: "the ability to see fine distinctions and differences." It's funny how far away that innocent, harmless, even fair definition takes us from the harsh reality of legal discrimination as a workplace issue.

In fiscal year 2008 alone, the Equal Employment Opportunity Commission (EEOC) reported that approximately $102.2 million was paid to resolve employment discrimination complaints. This includes claims under Title VII of the Civil Rights Act of 1964 (which is referred to simply as Title VII) for race and gender discrimination, as well as claims under statutes forbidding discrimination on the basis of disabilities, age, and gender. Those reported resolutions included only cases that were resolved in federal district courts with EEOC intervention. Therefore, that $102.2 million does not include the confidential, private settlements that companies and organizations pay to complaining parties.[1]

So what is discrimination under the legal concept of the term today? The basic federal law on employment discrimination includes the following:

■  Employment discrimination on the basis of race, color, religion, sex (gender), or national origin is prohibited by Title VII of the Civil Rights Act of 1964.

■  Employment discrimination is prohibited against qualified individuals with disabilities in the private sector, as well as state and local government, under the American with Disabilities Act of 1990 (ADA), with the same prohibition provided for federal employees with disabilities through the Rehabilitation Act of 1973.

■  Employment discrimination against individuals who are forty years of age or older is prohibited under the Age Discrimination Employment Act of 1967 (ADEA).

The federal government has other laws prohibiting job discrimination, but the ones listed above—though far from exhaustive—are among the laws that are most commonly known and frequently woven in with any meaningful discussion on the high price of paying attention to diversity issues in the workplace. Also, federal law does expand to catch up with society, so the list of protected classes grows. For example, the Genetic Information Nondiscrimination Act of 2008 prohibits discrimination on the basis of genetic information in health insurance and in hiring.

In addition, states, cities, and municipalities can include more groups to make a protected class, although they can't narrow federal legal protections. For example, as of this writing, the city of Kansas City, Missouri, prohibits discrimination on the basis of sexual orientation, although the state of Missouri and the federal government do not.

Although most people are generally familiar with the basics of *who* can't be discriminated against, many aren't aware of the broad scope of the *ways* that people can be discriminated against. The EEOC finds the following discriminatory practices over which an individual or group of individuals can make a claim of discrimination under Title VII, the ADA, or the ADEA:

- Hiring and firing

- Compensation, assignment, or classification of employees

- Transfer, promotion, layoff, or recall of employees

- Job advertisements

- Recruitment

- Testing

- Use of company facilities

- Training and apprenticeship programs

- Fringe benefits

- Pay, retirement plans, and disability leave

- Other terms and conditions of employment

The above list includes harassment on the basis of religion, gender, national origin, disability, or age or retaliation against an individual for filing a charge or participating in an investigation.

## How Does Antidiscrimination Differ from Diversity?

The dual concept of not discriminating legally against anyone and yet promoting diversity can be a really puzzling one—more so for those who are against promoting diversity since they often express fear that it is at the expense of "merit."

A handful of people have openly expressed to me that they thought diversity was a waste of time because if people just focused on work, then there did not need to be any special emphasis on whom you work with. One person in particular who said this to me was an older African-American male insurance agent who worked in an office by himself and had done so for most of the previous thirty years. He followed up this statement by saying that women who dressed too provocatively in the workplace were responsible for 80 percent of the problems involving workplace discrimination against women. He then followed up his social commentary by saying that if an employee openly mentioned that he was gay, he would immediately fire him on the spot because "there's no place for that in the workplace."

This example shows that diversity isn't just about accepting the people whom you find important or the differences you find worthy of acknowledgment. Instead, diversity deals with the cohesiveness and fairness of running an entire workforce.

Also, work has *never* just been about work. Work is about communication, interpersonal interaction, customer or client relationships, and managing people as well as the unofficial aspect of being able to get along with all kinds of people. Even as early as kindergarten, kids are socialized, judged, and graded on their ability to "play well with others." In the workplace, part of playing well with others means learning to cross the bridges that appear between one background or lifestyle or worldview and another—sometimes involving differences that can be diametrically opposed.

One of the reasons that diversity can be a difficult and controversial topic to discuss is that for every person who finds value and productivity in working with difference, there is someone who finds it disruptive and distracting from an organization's bottom line.

However, a study by Cedric Herring, professor of sociology at the University of Illinois at Chicago, suggests that diversity produces tangible benefits for a business. He found that racial diversity improved performance even after controlling for such factors as a company's legal form of organization, gender composition, size, age, type of work, and region. According to his analysis, average sales revenues of organizations with low racial diversity were approximately $3.1 million, compared with $3.9 million for those with medium diversity and $5.7 million for those with high diversity.[2]

No matter what you call it, diversity matters. If it makes you feel better to call it good manners, being P.C., or even Fred, it matters.

The insensitive comment that a new employee makes during his first week of work that gets repeated and circulated and retooled upon the telling helps create—or destroy—working relationships. This will impact his entire career at this place of business, no matter how perfect (not that anyone's work is ever perfect) his work may be.

It is true that once people arrive at work, work is fundamentally the most important issue there. But work is as much about the evaluation of how that work is done as any completely objective criteria that may exist for it.

Also, the assistance you get in doing a job often determines the quality of how the job is done. So employees getting along with other employees is no simple "feel good" concept that serves as a mere side issue to getting the job done. That's why managers and workplace leaders always have to be vigilant about the interpersonal issues that surround how the work gets done.

If you think it isn't important, ask a production worker who works down the line from two coworkers who can't get along. Ask two accountants who share a secretary in their office about how much discretion is used by the secretary to determine whose work gets done first, fastest, and best. And ask one of those accountants if bias or personal feelings ever factors into the discretion used by that secretary.

Even in jobs that are relatively solitary by nature, there's always a need or situation to remind the lone wolf that it's true that "no man (or woman) is an island."

## What Is a Protected Class and Is There Anyone Left Unprotected?

One of the biggest misunderstandings of employment discrimination is that there are some groups who can sue on the basis of discrimination and some who can't. For example, it is a false belief that racial minorities can sue for race discrimination against whites but that it's "reverse discrimination" when whites are discriminated against by minorities.

Technically, there is no "reverse discrimination" but rather discrimination on the basis of race regardless of the race of either the person claiming discrimination or the person accused of doing the unlawful discrimination. Another way of putting it is that it's not that some people have rights and others don't—it's that everyone has rights although not every status has a legal right.

If a white factory worker believes his black supervisor promotes only other blacks, then any claim he makes is on the basis of racial discrimination because he is saying that adverse employment decisions are based improperly on race. Does that mean that affirmative action is illegal? No, because affirmative action is about making sure there is a diverse pool of applicants to choose from. That's why the exact same logic would be at play if the supervisor was white and the complaining worker was black. Therefore, any claim of adverse action is legally just discrimination, never reverse discrimination, any more than East should be considered "reverse West" because of the direction you're looking in.

Of course, a 2009 ruling by the U.S. Supreme Court complicated the concept of what people think about reverse discrimination. In its 5–4 decision, the Court sided with a group of mostly white firefighters from the city of New Haven, Connecticut, ruling that the city improperly threw out the results of promotion exams after no minorities scored highly enough to be promoted. The Court ruled that the city made an impermissible legal finding on the basis of race under Title VII that created disparate impact, which means that a practice that on the surface looks neutral or fair actually creates an unfair and adverse impact on a legally protected group. Some lawyers view this ruling as really saying that disparate impact of a test on racial minorities is not, in itself, enough to "reasonably" conclude that the test illegally discriminates against minorities. These lawyers maintain that in order to throw out the test, the employer will have to point to some factors other than fear of getting sued. This ruling was viewed as an upholding of the "rights" of people in reverse discrimination cases. In my view, it's the Court enforcing the overall policy that it is illegal to have adverse employment decisions turn on issues of race.

Under the eyes of U.S. law, it's the basis on which you sue that determines whether you can bring a cause of action. The protected classes, in most jurisdictions, are race, national origin, gender, age, disability, and—in some jurisdictions—sexual orientation. Also, people can bring a discrimination case under Title VII because of their association with a member of a protected class. In other words, they are not alleging that they are being discriminated against because of their status but because of their association with or support for someone else who is being discriminated against because of his or her membership in a protected class.

Where this ties in with diversity is that discrimination is the concept of harming other people in the workplace based on their membership in a protected class that the law recognizes. Diversity is the attempt to expand positive understanding on the basis of both the legally protected classes and the groups not protected by law. And since everyone is in a legally protected class, diversity is about understanding exactly what that means and how to respect others.

One area that no jurisdiction considers a protected class is education. As a society, we've established that rewarding people who have higher education while looking less favorably on those without as much education is an acceptable way to distinguish one job candidate from another. Therefore, as long as the reason isn't pretext for discrimination that is covered by the law, a high school graduate could not sue an employer for discrimination for hiring a college graduate instead of him or her because education is not a legally protected class.

## Thoughts vs. Behavior

The law doesn't cover your thoughts in the workplace when it comes to workplace discrimination. Heck, the law doesn't really cover your behavior outside the workplace when it comes to your behavior in the workplace. But in the workplace, your behavior—the actual actions you take, discussions you initiate, words you say—are governed by the laws on employment discrimination and in most cases by company policy.

So if you, for example, as a male, have very distinct ideas about a woman's place and how she shouldn't be in the workplace—especially if she has children to raise or makes more money than the men—because that violates your personal or moral code, that is perfectly all right. It is your absolute right to hold that opinion. It's certainly your right to have an agreement with the women in your personal life to live up to those expectations and that belief system.

However, the second you voice that opinion at work, making the environment uncomfortable for your female employees, that's when your thoughts and opinions do matter. They also matter if you let your opinions govern an employment decision you make that affects even one women in any way, shape, or form. And your thoughts and opinions matter if they lead to any action or inaction that causes a negative employment outcome for a woman. What's more, if any complaint against you goes far enough—for example, if literally a federal case is made—then even those outside choices and lifestyle opinions and behaviors that didn't matter before suddenly become evidence used to demonstrate that your motivation in the workplace was deliberately discriminatory.

Now, on some level, one could argue that thoughts are important because they lay the foundation from which all actions and behaviors spring. That's why the topic of diversity remains a vital issue in the workplace, because exposing people to understanding the backgrounds of other people forms the start in getting people to think a little differently. Thinking a little differently helps a person to do things a little differently, which results in a lot fewer people discriminating on the basis of ignorance. There will always exist people who deliberately and willfully discriminate despite knowing better. But that's beyond the scope of what people who care about diversity can do anything about.

## Keys to Breaking This Chapter's Code

■ Avoiding lawsuits and discrimination complaints is a motivating factor for having a diverse and inclusive workplace.

■ Federal, state, and local governments have specific reasons under which no American can be discriminated against. The most common prohibitions are on the basis of race, gender, age, disability, and religion.

■ The concept of protected classes protects everyone from discrimination, not just minority group members.

## Diversity Exercise

Either verbally to yourself or on a separate piece of paper (but not in this book, not on your computer, and not on any piece of paper that isn't immediately destroyed), admit to five biases that you have that you would not want to admit if you were standing at a podium in front of your entire workforce at a company retreat.

Pick biases that make even *you* uncomfortable, not "should" biases that make you feel good, like "I'm biased against other employees who don't give work their best effort."

Get raw. Get real with yourself.

Maybe your list of five real biases looks something like this:

- "I'm biased against people who smoke."

- "I'm biased against the grossly overweight."

- "I'm biased against people who speak with accents."

- "I'm biased against people who flaunt their sexual orientation."

- "I'm biased against people who have visible tattoos."

This is a hard exercise, but if you can think of even one time when someone's difference made you uncomfortable or annoyed you, include it on your list.

## Notes

1.  U.S. Equal Employment Opportunity Commission, Enforcement Statistics and Litigation, http://www.eeoc.gov/eeoc/statistics/enforcement/litigation.cfm.

2.  Cedric Herring, "Does Diversity Pay? Race, Gender, and the Business Case for Diversity." *American Sociological Review,* April 2009.

# CHAPTER FOUR

# How Do Diversity Issues Differ from Discrimination?

*Dear Diversity Diva:*

*Shouldn't you really be called "Discrimination Diva"? I mean, seriously, isn't that all you're really writing about? As a manager, it seems that it is about encouraging a bunch of people to whine and complain because they don't get their way in the workplace by getting the company all worked up about diversity.*

*Signed,*
*Dumbing Down Diversity Discussion*

## Harmony vs. Harm

In dealing with difference as a purely legal requirement, the issue always rests on harm and if harm is created. The law doesn't care about whether workers are happy, unified, motivated, or operating at their best. The law just wants to make sure that no one is harmed in any of the ways that we as a society have generally mandated should not happen in the workplace.

It's like our traffic laws. The law doesn't mandate whether you get to drive a new luxury car or a broken down eyesore or what stores you are allowed to drive your car to. But the law does mandate the speed at which you drive, the places where you have to slow down or stop, and—in some jurisdictions—the basic condition your car has to be in to even drive on public streets.

But diversity is different. It's about harmony. It's about creating an environment where people can work and feel that fairness can coexist with differences. With diversity, while individual feelings may not matter, collective understanding does. Diversity also has the goal of creating an environment where no harm takes place because of difference. But at its best, a good workplace diversity initiative focuses more on promoting understanding and cohesiveness than it does on merely being a prophylactic for discrimination.

## Affirmative Action as a Complementary Issue

One of the reasons that people mistakenly tie issues of diversity to race and gender is because many individuals link diversity with affirmative action, and affirmative action is a very specific (and controversial) legal remedy to address past and current societal discrimination that has resulted in an unfairly imbalanced workforce. By "imbalanced," I refer to a workforce that—at least in terms of race and gender—has been composed by a society that legally allowed hiring based on race and gender and did not prohibit firings, unfair promotions, or outright inequity of treatment based on race and gender and several other non–work-related factors such as disability, pregnancy, age, or religion.

The workforce that has evolved over time from our past society—in terms of people with the most seniority, the grandest job titles, and the most significant positions of power, influence, and authority—would definitely have a different composition if an open and fair workplace had existed at all points of U.S. history.

This is not to say that the white men who disproportionately have these high and significant positions and benefited from this society do not deserve them. Opportunity often shapes success. The top white male CEOs of any Fortune 500 company from thirty years ago, for example, probably would have still done very well for themselves in terms of status and success even with a larger playing field of competitors. Many of them very well might have had these positions because their talent, hard work, and many other strengths and qualities would have placed them in that same exact spot. However, they just might not all have become CEOs.

But what if opportunity had been accessible to all people at all times and places of U.S. history? There is no telling how far up the ladder of companies women, people of different races, or other "outsiders" to leadership with even more talent, a higher work ethic, and more innovative strengths and qualities would have been propelled.

A study conducted several years ago researched how minority students admitted to the University of Michigan Law School under affirmative action succeeded years after graduation, compared to the rest of their graduating class. The study found that in all the measurements examined—which included jobs, money, honors, and contributions to their respective communities—the minority students admitted under affirmative action did as well as their peers.[1]

One of the criticisms of affirmative action is that a second wrong doesn't correct the first wrong. In other words, attempting to use race and gender as a factor in correcting historical societal wrongs is no more fair or equitable than the existence of the mind-set that created those conditions in the first place.

But there's a huge difference, and that difference is the basis for the misunderstanding. The first wrong made it legal to lawfully prevent entire groups of people from getting certain jobs and gave them no protection from being poorly and unfairly paid and treated in the jobs they did get. Affirmative action is about increasing the pool of people to choose from in selecting those who will be hired for jobs to help even the discrepancy from the decades of inequity.

The motivation for affirmative action does not hinge on any group of people being inferior, which was the motivation behind discrimination and kept entire groups of people from consideration prior to employment laws being put into place. In addition, affirmative action—true affirmative action—is not about the ultimate hiring decisions. That's an illegal quota. Rather, affirmative action is about purposefully taking action to create a diverse hiring pool so that over time, we have a shot at creating a fair and diverse workforce—a workforce that actually reflects society and the communities in which companies are based.

Therefore, that's when you know true affirmative action is actually working: when if, from a pool of diverse and qualified candidates, the best person is picked. And if that qualified person who is picked is a white male, then affirmative action has still done its job. Why? Because if every hiring pool in an organization is always authentically diverse, then the best qualified candidates chosen over time will cover a range of backgrounds. As a group or for the individuals within the group, white heterosexual males without disabilities are not always going to be the candidates with the best, most relevant credentials.

## Diversity Is to Affirmative Action What a Full-Service Auto Shop Is to a Single Gas Pump

Affirmative action is a narrow legal remedy—one that someday won't exist any more and whose past existence will seem as archaic and quaint but groundbreaking as the Gutenberg printing press or Ford's first car. But the need for diversity, and the need to value and understand and work with differences that people bring to the plate, will always exist.

When I think of diversity, I think of *Star Trek*—how in the future, the races on planet Earth have learned to get along and meld different backgrounds and cultures into a mosaic of talents, but we still reenact the same misunderstandings and hard stances, only on an intergalactic front with different species that have really different colors.

Humans seem hard-wired to distinguish and categorize other humans. If we just left it at identifying differences—the way we know the color purple isn't orange or a rose isn't an orchid—it would be one thing. But humans have come up with the nice little twist of taking our ability to distinguish and turning it into judging. When we judge, we weigh the differences and then view one set of people as having more value than another comparable set. And when it comes to work, we feel that we have the right to judge because it's all about getting the job done, right?

Diversity isn't always comfortable, but it's critical. It's about people learning to appreciate the way others are different, but not just in the ways where there appears to be legal emphasis.

The following categories aren't exhaustive but are among the most expansive ways diversity should be viewed:

- Race
- National origin
- English as a second (or third or more) language
- Gender
- Sexual orientation
- Age
- Physical and mental abilities and disabilities
- Religion
- Height

- Weight

- Looks

- Education

- Regional differences

- Socioeconomic class

- Value systems

- Work habits

- Marital and family status

Differences can range from the ingrained ways of thinking that define how a person views the world to the mundane but potentially disruptive differences, such as whether you're the type of work mate who makes a new pot of coffee after drinking the last cup or walks away leaving it for someone else to do.

Even those who work in a place where they believe all the races get along (again, resorting to the habitual tendency to view diversity only through the lens of race relations) can run down in detail all the different personality types that can make the workplace either a very annoying or a very enriching place to go every day. Therefore, when you have a five-minute conversation at the watercooler with the close-talking coworker whom everyone else avoids like the H1N1 flu, congratulate yourself for attempting to promote a diverse workforce.

## Receptivity: The First Step in Dealing with Diversity

Receptivity means that you have to be willing to see differences and not just the differences that you feel comfortable with.

That's easier said than done because what often happens is that people think that because they believe they have one big-ticket item in diversity down, it covers them like a blanket. An example would be blacks who believe that because they get along with whites at work, they have a good grasp on racial diversity despite the fact that they are clueless or worse in dealing with Hispanics, Asians, Native Americans, or members of any other racial group they work beside. Another example is people who think that because they are friendly with one "gay guy" at work, they have a firm grasp on all things gay and lesbian, despite having no idea about the difference between bisexual and transgender individuals.

Receptivity is about keeping your eyes open to the ways people show differences in the workplace. This is not necessarily so that you can fully understand every difference or grasp the nuance of every background but so that you can have the awareness to know when someone else's viewpoint or approach to a workplace issue might part company with yours.

## The Next Step in Handling Workplace Diversity Is Gauging Your Compassion

In a diversity workshop I conducted, there was a diversity exercise in which the participants discussed the issue of a hypothetical gay employee having to hide that he was gay as part of mentioning that he had missed work because of his sick life partner. One of the workshop participants said that the man should keep any information that he was gay out of the workplace because the information was personal and had absolutely no place in the work environment. This participant had mentioned earlier and with great pride that he was the divorced dad of three school-age kids to whom he was exceptionally devoted.

When I asked him how he would feel about working for an employer that required him to keep the existence of his children a secret, he got visibly angry, failing to see where I was going. He went on at passionate length about how he would quit a job that required him to deny the existence of his children because that would be outrageous, unreasonable, and unfair, and he could never do that to his children.

Clearly, he could not make the compassionate mental and emotional leap of putting himself in another's place based on his own life and priorities. However, from the looks on the faces of everyone else in the workshop (along with some uncomfortable squirming), it was clear that they were able to look at the example through the eyes of compassion.

The dictionary definition of *compassion* is "the humane quality of understanding the suffering of others and wanting to do something about it." For purposes of workplace diversity, I think it's enough to shorten the definition to "the humane quality of understanding others" as the least of how everyone can best navigate all the different kinds of "others" that going to work requires.

## Practicing Patience

When it comes to workplace diversity, patience is learning to manage that uncomfortable space of not knowing exactly how to deal with every difference or every challenge regarding diversity that comes along.

It's funny to me that diversity has the reputation of being a touchy-feely, soft issue that isn't a *real* issue in the workplace except for the HR department. In fact, problems erupt in the workplace because the clash of differences can be one of the most destructive and dismantling problems a company ever deals with.

Any employer, for example, who has ever had a disabled employee complain because other workers were unable to understand and accept the reasonable accommodation made available to him knows the importance of patience in getting others to understand what their minds seem closed to.

People just don't like to be uncomfortable. Even the most open-minded, freethinking individuals tense up when confronted with a difference that is completely out of their toolbox of experiences and thoughts. I think in that case that the open-minded can be even more resistant to admitting their resistance.

It takes a lot of patience to choose to recognize a difference and then allow yourself to understand it. It takes patience, for example, to live in a city and work in an environment where referring to people as only Hispanic or Latino just doesn't cut it—one where you need to know the cultural differences between someone from Mexico or Puerto Rico or El Salvador or Cuba or Spain. And in those instances, that's dealing with broad cultural differences and distinctions.

Patience will also be at play when you have to work the first time for a female supervisor who doesn't understand the framework you've come to associate with working for a woman. You know, the framework that you think you've thoughtfully adopted from years of experience and observation. The one that you think is unbiased and certainly is not a stereotype—only now you're confronted with someone who is not in the box, which is very irritating because it was such a tidy, well-constructed box.

That's when you need patience—to help you get past the learning curve of needing to deal with that which you don't know, because the learning curve never goes away. It just pops up in unexpected times and places.

## Keys to Breaking This Chapter's Code

- Affirmative action works to eliminate harm based on differences, while the true point of diversity is creating harmony.

- Affirmative action is a single, imperfect tool that aims, over time, to level out the playing field of access to equal opportunity.

- The keys to dealing with diversity as a workplace issue are receptivity, compassion, and patience.

## Diversity Exercise

I'm not trying to encourage anyone to walk around thinking of how to become a plaintiff in a lawsuit, but I want you to look at the following checklist and determine if you are in a protected class since the purpose of this exercise is for you to see that *everyone* is in a protected class, not just historically disadvantaged groups:

- Race

- Color

- Gender

- Age, but only if you are over the age of forty

- Disability

With the exception of disability or age if you're under forty, you should have been able to list yourself as being in a protected class for each one of these categories. If you are white, for example, it doesn't mean that you are not a member of a protected class when it comes to the category of race. If you are male, for example, it doesn't mean that you are not a member of a protected class when it comes to gender.

## Note

1.    Richard O. Lempert, David L. Chambers, and Terry K. Adams, "Michigan's Minority Graduates in Practice: The River Runs Through Law School." *Law & Social Inquiry,* April 2000.

# CHAPTER FIVE

# Shouldn't I Just Have to Worry About What the Law Requires Me to Worry About?

*Dear Diversity Diva:*

*Girlfriend, could you just bottom-line it for me? Tell me what the law is on diversity or discrimination or whatever and that's what I'll do or won't do, and as a manager I'll make sure that my people won't do it either.*

*Signed,*
*Doing Only What I Need to Do*

## Don't I Just Have to Pay Attention to the Law?

As I have said in several different ways throughout this book, the law is very limited in what it addresses when it comes to diversity. Legal prohibitions are about telling people what they can't do. True diversity and inclusion in the workplace is about enhancing the workplace in the ways the law can't enforce.

The law can say that it's actionable if you create a hostile work environment based on one of the legally defined protected classes. But the law doesn't address the ways in which you create a positive environment—through diversity initiatives, workshops, affinity or human resource groups, and the small and large personal interactions that help compose a workplace.

## The Changing Faces of Diversity

One of the first and most important topics covered in diversity workshops is why diversity is important in the first place. The most obvious reason that people start with is the changing demographics of the United States and its workforce. The U.S. Census Bureau predicts that by the year 2042, the workplace will find white Americans in the racial minority for the first time. Some states are already seeing that demographic shift. In 2009, according to the Census Bureau, 53 percent of the population in Texas was minority, and 58 percent of the populations of California and New Mexico were minorities.

Globally, diversity in terms of ethnicity alone is wider and more intricate than we think of it in the United States. In other words, where race is concerned in the United States, whites are the majority, but that's not the case in the global community. According to statistics from the United Nations, the United States makes up less than 5 percent of the world population, while China and India combined are almost 37 percent and Africa is about 12 percent.

As everyone knows, race and gender are the most visible and talked about elements of diversity. That's why, to the extent that discrimination claims are filed, race- and gender-based complaints are the two largest kinds filed with the EEOC. For example, in fiscal year 2008, out of all discrimination lawsuits filed, 33,937 complaints were filed on the basis of race and 28,372 complaints were filed on the basis of gender discrimination. One reason why race and gender represent such a large number of complaints is because both are categories that everyone is a member of in some way. (Everyone has a race or gender, but not everyone necessarily has a disability or is old enough to legally bring an age discrimination claim, for example.) Also, both are areas that people can readily identify in another.

But past race and gender, the reason why diversity is important is that as the population grows, the number of different kinds of people entering the workforce changes. Therefore, in learning to deal with difference, a company also learns to deal with change, and a company that can deal with change is better positioned to make moves and steps that keep it in alignment with a constantly morphing global economy.

On an international level, the nuances among countries, cultures, and races can be striking, and failure to honor the nuances can be detrimental to business. Whereas we in the United States get very concerned about labeling behavior as stereotypical, on a global level, differences are just that—differences.

The website www.WorldBusinessCulture.com does a great job giving guidelines on how to handle various differences from country to country. For example, in China, generally speaking, one should expect long meetings that appear to have no clear objectives, while in Germany, strong debate is encouraged and expected at meetings.

When it comes to the cultural nuances between countries, people in other nations and parts of the world tend to be much more comfortable with acknowledging differences. In the United States, though, cultural differences—particularly those involving race—can be much more sensitive and thus, unacknowledged.

## Most Issues Don't Rise to the Level of the Law

Most challenges regarding diversity in the workplace don't rise to the level of an EEOC complaint, a lawsuit, or even a trip to the HR department. For many in the workplace, issues of diversity—sometimes even outright discrimination—remain personal issues that aren't treated as personnel issues.

The awkwardness that a man with an accent faces in the workplace, the seething annoyance a black employee feels over his marginalized status, and the frustration a working mother feels over her company policies regarding time off often do not turn into formal complaints. Rather, they turn into whispered conversations by the watercooler or the coffeepot, heated reenactments of offensive past comments made, and passive-aggressive responses to deadlines and rules. Eventually, they turn into a request for a transfer to another department or the person's finding another job out of the company altogether.

Sometimes, a discrimination complaint filed by one employee is nothing more than a patchwork quilt of complaints stitched together from the complaints that other similar employees have had—events and comments that people have talked about on the sly for quite some time.

## Change Keeping Up with Change

Another reason why diversity as an overarching issue is an important priority to grasp is because change changes. Here's a partial list of things we did not see, say, back in the 1960s: blacks and Hispanics and Asians and Native Americans in office jobs; openly gay and lesbian men and women; people with disabilities, along with the accommodations that went with their particular needs; pregnant women as managers; and never married or divorced parents freely discussing the children they worked to support.

With change comes more change. And even though the levels of diversity aren't handled in a singular, formulaic way, the habit of dealing with differences in ways that involve receptivity, compassion, and patience doesn't change. Even when groups and cultural dynamics can be grasped, the nuances of them shift, and certainly the individual situations can and do change.

It's like learning to cook. Making an omelet requires different skills than baking a cake, but the ease and familiarity you get from being in the kitchen make it easier to take on trying a whole new dish.

## Denial Can't Deny the Reality of Others

One of the most tragically disappointing aspects of discussing diversity is how quickly open, engaging conversation can shut down. Quite frequently, when people from an underrepresented group in the workplace issue an opinion about how something affects them based on their status in that group, a negative reaction of rejection is triggered among others in the workplace—kneejerk defensiveness, if you will.

Say Pete, who is visually impaired, comments to Frank about how Leo seems uncomfortable dealing with him because of his disability. Since Frank does not have a disability, he finds himself having the kneejerk reaction to defend Leo and deny that Leo feels uncomfortable with Pete's disability.

A couple of dynamics come into play here. Pete most likely will be irritated that Frank has completely discounted that there is even a slight possibility that he is correct that Leo is uncomfortable dealing with Pete because of Pete's disability. Frank, on the other hand—on a level that he may not even be aware of—may identify more with Leo in that neither of them is disabled. Therefore, Frank may automatically defend Leo because a part of him feels that he is being lumped into the same category and he would never want Pete to say that about him. So, in denying Leo's feelings to Pete, Frank is trying to make sure that he too is not perceived as globally guilty. Another possibility is that Frank is just oblivious to what Pete is talking about because he can't relate to Pete's life circumstance. However, it's important to understand that for someone in Pete's position who does live these issues every day, the specific reason for Frank's automatic defense of Leo may not really matter, and Pete could take Frank's defense of Leo as also being insensitive to Pete's feelings.

Regardless of the reason, most of people's instinctive defending of others who seem similarly situated to themselves happens in the blink of an eye. The herd mentality creeps in before they have even consciously identified that they consider themselves the same kind of animal as the person being talked about.

Minority group members can get aggravated at how quickly their defense of members of their group gets reduced to "you're just defending your own." A lot of times, though, that's exactly true. People are just defending their own. What is also exactly true is that majority group members do the exact same thing, only with less conscious awareness of doing so, thus oftentimes labeling their opinions as being "objective."

As an employment attorney, I found that juries, including mock juries, found it far easier to come up with a verdict for retaliation rather than discrimination in cases where both discrimination and retaliation claims were made. My theory is that people greatly resist wanting to believe that someone can or actually does discriminate in the workplace on the basis of something an employee can't control, such as race or gender or disability. But they can wrap their minds around an employer wanting to "get even" with an employee who brings a claim or stirs up the workplace waters.

Even when the denial is about a complete stranger or an event in the news, denial and failure to want to acknowledge the other perspective can be at play. It's almost like the person, in denying it, is saying, "If I acknowledge the possibility [that something is unfairly happening to someone on the basis of some group she is a member of], then I'm acknowledging that it could be true, and I don't want to give this group of people the power to make me or people like me the bad guys."

Once, a white woman in her late sixties that I had a friendly working relationship with called me "prejudiced" because of the columns on race relations I had written earlier that year in our local newspaper. When I probed her on what exactly it was that I had written that prompted her conclusion, she admitted that it wasn't anything I wrote so much as that she felt uncomfortable hearing that others were facing issues of inequity, because she didn't want to believe it still happened. That's an example of making a judgment on someone else's observation to stamp out your internal discomfort.

In the situation illustrated above by Pete, Frank, and Leo, the potential problem isn't all Frank's fault. Sometimes, when people who are in the minority group of a situation raise an issue, the point of bringing it to someone who isn't walking in that group's shoes has to be examined.

The assumption shouldn't be that only people who are exactly in your shoes understand the road you're walking. But at the same time, if you don't know that the person you're talking to has a pertinent frame of reference for understanding your point—especially in the workplace, where these issues can take on additional weight and meaning—then you might be setting yourself up for a defensive reaction. Similarly, the person you're talking to might have a frame of reference that is equally pertinent but different from yours.

So, what could Frank have done differently in our scenario? He could have taken a couple of different approaches, neither of which is inherently defensive. Frank could have said something along the lines of, "Really? I've never noticed that about Leo, but now that you've brought it to my attention, I'll see if I notice it in the future." Or if Frank was genuinely interested, he could have asked questions. Even one "What makes you think that?" goes a long way toward building a bridge of understanding.

Even if Frank's gut instinct signals to him that what Pete is saying isn't true—maybe because Frank knows Leo better than Pete knows Leo, and Frank just doesn't believe that what Pete says is what is going on—unless Frank thinks that Pete is a liar or is crazy, Frank should respect that there is some reason why Pete holds that opinion about Leo.

The advantage to handling it this way is that Pete feels heard, and maybe Frank (if he is in a position to) can help steer this issue in the right direction by tactfully alerting Leo to behavior that Leo may be unintentionally exhibiting that leaves Pete with his perception.

What could Pete have done differently in this situation? Pete could have honestly asked himself if Frank was really the best person to share his concern with. Also, if Pete decided to share his observation with Frank anyway, he might have been prepared to give specific examples and reasons upon which his opinion was based, rather than just sharing the conclusion, especially since it was such a damaging one. He could also ask why Frank thought Leo acts the way he does. Perhaps there is something else going on that Frank may shed some light on, and Pete should be open to that as well.

Discussing the perceived biases of others at work can lead to a dangerous interaction—one where speaking cautiously and listening objectively are required on both sides of the conversation.

## Keys to Breaking This Chapter's Code

- Knowing employment laws is only one aspect of understanding diversity.

- Most problems that people have regarding diversity never even make it to the point of an official complaint or lawsuit.

- Denying the reality of others can be one of the quickest ways to short-circuit understanding and can contribute to perceptions snowballing out of control. This applies to both sets of perceptions. Be prepared to challenge your own assumptions and frame of reference.

## Diversity Exercise

This will probably be the most difficult exercise in the book, except for the people who read everything anyway. Go find the poster in your workplace that you've walked past a thousand times explaining your workplace rights regarding employment and discrimination and read every word. Yep, every word.

Since it probably is near where you get your coffee or microwave your food, read it then. You can cheat by breaking up the reading into multiple sessions—maybe one paragraph for every cup of coffee poured or every frozen meal microwaved for lunch.

Read it all? Exercise done.

The purpose of this exercise is for you to read what the law actually covers and what it doesn't even address, since most people aren't as knowledgeable about discrimination law as they think they are and thus, they may be surprised to find that it covers much less than they think it does. Some people, on the other hand, may find that it covers much more.

# CHAPTER SIX

# Why Isn't It Enough to Just Acknowledge the Ways in Which People Are the Same?

*Dear Diversity Diva:*

*I think there's something wrong with you. Aren't you encouraging us to be judgmental bigots by even noticing how people are different? Shouldn't we just concentrate on the ways people are alike?*

*Signed,*
*Simpler to Be the Same*

## The Opposite of Bad Is Not Oblivious

Oftentimes the approach that many attempt to take in dealing with diversity is to act like differences don't exist—after all, if you don't notice differences, you can never be accused of treating people differently or harboring prejudice, can you? But treating people as if they are all the same is actually the single-handedly rudest thing you can do. Okay, maybe "rude" is a little harsh, but it is definitely insensitive. People mistakenly think that noticing a difference is the same as judging a difference. It isn't, and people don't like to feel as if their uniqueness—a different way of perceiving diversity— is being ignored.

It reminds me of a conversation I heard while listening to Bill O'Reilly's radio show and some issue of race came up. O'Reilly made the statement that he didn't notice the race of people when they walked into a room. The person on the air challenged him on that point, and in classic Bill O'Reilly fashion, he held stubbornly to his position. The person, who apparently was reading my mind, then asked O'Reilly if he noticed when a woman entered a room, which prompted O'Reilly to avoid answering the question by joking that it depended on whether the woman was attractive or not. The point was a great one because it almost always sounds disingenuous to people when you say you don't know how someone differs from everyone else in a situation. Again, the issue isn't judging the difference, having an emotional reaction to the difference, or even finding the difference worth commenting on. It is just merely being aware of the difference.

People are individuals, and individuals are not various-sized flesh bags carrying bones and blood. One of the hang-ups of truly grasping and appreciating diversity without being mired in resentfulness is viewing diversity as the highest form of honoring individualism. That might sound contrary, but only because diversity has become synonymous with political correctness, which constantly pits one group against another in deciding the ways and means of how to treat others.

But think about how an advertising executive who was raised on a farm and grew up with literally no modern or electronic conveniences might look at how to advertise a new product, compared to his coworker who was raised by high-income suburban parents who bought every technological innovation before the first-generation prototype could be perfected. Those two executives, while similarly educated, of roughly the same age, and with practically the identical professional pedigree of experiences, most likely view the same project with remarkably different perspectives.

> LIFELONG TECHIE: Let's have a commercial where we have this little boy milking a cow one night …

> BORN FARMER (interrupting): You don't milk cows at night.

> LIFELONG TECHIE: Whatever. Anyway, for the commercial it will look better to have a full moon in the background.

> BORN FARMER: That's great that you want the full moon backdrop but you don't milk cows at night.

> Lifelong Techie rolls his eyes.

These two ad execs are having a culture clash that has a distinct impact on their work. The clash doesn't stem from color, race, gender, sexual orientation, or any of the issues that people typically leap to when thinking about diversity. But that's exactly what this is.

In the context of diversity, one of my favorite definitions of culture comes from the 1990 book *Flow: The Psychology of Optimal Experience* by Mihaly Csikszentmihalyi. He writes, "Cultures are defensive constructions against chaos, designed to reduce the impact of randomness on experience."[1] In other words, culture is the shorthand way I choose to view the world around me by basing it on what I already know and feel comfortable with.

Cultural clash can be as simple as one person who grows up with a different way of life from another person and is protective about the representation of facts and his upbringing. In this sentence, the word "culture" or "background" could be substituted for "upbringing," but they all boil down to the same thing.

The clash between a farm boy and a tekkie may not be governed by law or even company policy, but it is an illustration of how we can't look at two people and rub out their differences because it's more convenient to focus on their similarities.

Even when there isn't a radical difference in backgrounds—such as with the person raised on a farm without exposure to modern conveniences versus someone raised in electronic overload—there can be a radical difference in perspective that defies concrete reason.

During the national election season of 2008, for example, a narrow-minded person may have assumed that any black supporting Barack Obama merely voted for him because he would be the first black president of the United States. But there are blacks who didn't vote for Obama at all, blacks who voted for him only because he beat the person they voted for in the Democratic primary, blacks who voted for him because they always vote for Democrats, blacks who voted for him because they despised the opposition, blacks who voted for him because of his stance on specific issues, and yes, blacks whose sole reason for voting for Obama was because he too was black.

The flip of that point, however, would be saying that every white person who did not vote for Obama voted for John McCain because McCain is white—even if the voter always voted Republican or specifically supported certain political positions that Obama didn't support. See why you have to be careful about reductionist analysis based on race or any other category of membership? Because it's one that can always be flipped completely around to take you down a different illogical and insulting road.

## Our Society and Differences

Often, people who proclaim their desire to not see difference hold that viewpoint about the differences that deep down aren't that important to them. However, they see difference all the time in situations where they do hold a strong opinion. For example, a person who grew up as the oldest child can see very well how that makes him different from his youngest sibling. A person who holds several degrees from academia can see how she may have a different view on higher taxes to build a new library in her community than an individual coming from a background where education wasn't respected and thus, no one in the family chose to go further than partway through high school. People always see differences; we can just be selective about the ones we choose to acknowledge.

## Siblings, Parents, and Friends

Most people have had multiple associations in their lives—parents, grandparents, siblings, friends—long before they enter the workforce. And most people would never treat their loved ones without making distinctions.

You may love your mother and father equally, but there aren't too many people who would buy their parents the exact same gift for their respective birthdays, major gift-giving holidays, or Mother's and Father's Days (outside of buying a joint gift for both of them). It's the same thing regarding siblings. Except for the rare year when you give all your siblings the exact same thing for whatever reason, you make a distinction, whether it's taking into account their tastes, their interests, their current life situations, their experiences, or even your relationship with them at the time you're giving the gift.

Therefore, when people talk about treating everyone the same, that's never really the case because we make distinctions in our personal lives starting before we're old enough to crawl across a room.

At a diversity workshop for firefighters, I facilitated this very issue in the context of saving lives. The workshop was made up of all white men except for one Hispanic man and one black man. One firefighter asked why people shouldn't just be treated exactly the same. After all, wouldn't that be the simplest, most fair way to treat everyone?

I pointed out that when they go to the scene of a fire and have to make decisions on how to get people out safely, there is probably a difference in how they rescue a healthy, physically strong sixteen-year-old boy who is not incapacitated by smoke, fire, or injury, as opposed to how they rescue a frail, eighty-one-year-old woman with obvious physical ailments. The firefighters got my point that sometimes the most fair and just thing you can do in your treatment of others takes into account their different circumstances or conditions so that you can treat them with the same and equal degree of respect, dignity, and compassion.

The firefighters could get the point easily when it came to the split-second decisions of life and death that their job required. But, like most of us, the seemingly noncritical and more leisurely decisions regarding difference seem much harder to understand and navigate.

## Keys to Breaking This Chapter's Code

- Being oblivious to the differences of others doesn't make you more respectful—rather, less so in many cases.

- Noticing a difference is not the same as judging a difference, let alone having a negative judgment.

- We make distinctions in our personal lives all the time and don't have any problem with doing so. Workplace diversity just requires you to use the same dispassionate compassion.

## Diversity Exercise

Pick someone in your workplace who is as close as possible to you judging by obvious, visible characteristics such as race, gender, age, and any disabilities you may have. If at all possible, pick someone whom you know a lot about.

Now, make two lists on a piece of paper—one about you and one about the person you selected. List absolutely every difference you can think of, getting downright picky if you need to. Look at things like marital status, number of children, number of siblings, number of pets, types of pets, parts of the country you grew up in, parts of the community you live in now, general religious or spiritual practices, the ways you dress, eating tastes, hobbies, health habits, kinds of things you read, workplace habits, and talking styles.

At the end of the exercise (hopefully), you'll see how individuals can be very different despite that fact that people view race and gender as the only elements of diversity people tend to take note of.

## Group Exercise

Have everyone take some interest or aspect of their life and write down the ways it is a culture within itself. Then everyone should share the aspects of that culture with the rest of the group. Try to have people stay away from broad groups like racial membership, but they can use groups that involve race if they want. For example, rather than having a black person explain the culture of "being black," have him explain the culture of being in local black skiers groups. Or rather than have someone describe the culture of "being Christian," have her identify the specific culture of the church she attends. The point of the exercise is to show how people create cultures for themselves in addition to the ones that they are naturally a part of, and those cultures cover a range of details and habits that an "outsider" would have trouble figuring out at first.

## Note

1.    Mihaly Csikszentmihalyi, *Flow: The Psychology of Optimal Experience* (New York: Harper Perennial, 1990).

# Doesn't Figuring Out Everybody's Differences at Work Take Too Much Time Away from Work?

*Dear Diversity Diva:*

*I go to work to work, not to make friends. Instead of worrying about diversity and differences and getting along with and understanding people, shouldn't I just be doing my job as a manager? Shouldn't I just be paying attention to how the people I manage do theirs? Aren't you asking me to do more than they pay me to do?*

*Signed,*
*I Work Hard for the Money*

## Familiarity Breeds Comfort, Liking, and Trust

In an ideal world, people wouldn't have to worry about getting along with other people. But the world has never been ideal.

There are many things that modern man and woman had to learn to do. (Programming a DVR and multitasking while driving on the highway come to mind.) Accepting differences and not perceiving them as a threat should be added to that list. If we can accept differences and learn about other people, we will not have to make assumptions about others when we don't have the facts to fill in all the blanks.

Sometimes, we are thrown off base when things are not the way we assumed they would be. For example, a study by psychologists found that when participants began talking with an Asian-American woman and discovered that she had a Southern accent, they showed a spike in blood pressure. The psychologists hypothesized that the rise in blood pressure was a response to the surprise and cognitive dissonance of having to navigate an unexpected occurrence of this nature, which makes it more "threatening."[1]

Antonio Damasio, a professor of psychology and neuroscience and director of the Brain and Creativity Institute at the University of Southern California, has said that detection of differences has a biological history, where it was advantageous to recognize differences rapidly to anticipate how to react to a different group that might be unfriendly. Damasio makes the point, however, that while there may be biological explanations for why we recognize differences, our responses were created by the perceived circumstances.

I believe that the perception of difference, especially in workplace situations, does require constant awareness because of the natural—biological—tendency to have "dis-ease" when dealing with the differences of others. On a positive note, studies of how we perceive differences show that familiarity and friendship decreases the physical response to members of a different group in terms of being a threat.

According to Brian Lickel, a social psychologist at the University of Southern California, "One finding that's becoming clear is that friendships are absolutely key. When you form friendships with people of different ethnic backgrounds—that appears to have a big effect on your general attitude about people belonging to that group." [2]

In some situations, however, before people can even contemplate friendship, they have to get past the initial discomfort they are confronted with in the presence of the differences of others. For example, in the part of the Midwest where I grew up and now live, it's common to find walk-in nail salons owned and run by Asians who speak little to no English, other than basic transactional conversation. What's almost as common are the comments from customers who hate that the workers don't speak English. The customers assume that the workers are all sitting around talking about them.

When I hear those comments, I respond by saying, "So, what if they are?" So what if people who are speaking in a language that you don't understand anyway are talking about you, as long as they are giving you good service at a fair price and no other problems come up? I then point out (and yes, it's amazing that I have a lot of friends after saying things like this) how arrogant it is for them to assume that a group of people who all know each other, either by family ties or work ties, have nothing better to talk about than the strangers coming in for a manicure or pedicure.

For those customers who insist that they know the workers are making rude comments in their native tongue, I suggest the solutions of either learning to speak the language or finding another nail salon where the workers make insults behind your back in a language you can actually understand. Regardless, language isn't the real issue.

Jumping to conclusions and having cultural arrogance often go hand-in-hand. It is understandable that you might feel uncomfortable in situations where people are speaking a different language and could be talking about you. But this doesn't have to be a response that you feel entitled to have, especially in situations where you are choosing to do business with people whose first language is not English.

## It's Not a Full-Time Job to Know the People Who Do Their Jobs Around You

At its heart, diversity is as much about listening and asking questions as it is about talking and disclosing. By asking questions, I don't mean examining people as if you were a lawyer taking a deposition or a zoologist investigating the characteristics of some exotic new animal.

Instead, asking questions starts by having real, everyday conversations with people in benign circumstances about truly innocent topics and going from there. Sometimes just asking people what they did over the weekend when you're all pouring coffee on Monday morning leads to finding out something about them. The next time you all talk, asking a question that is relevant to diversity becomes easier and more natural because something related may have already come up in conversation.

For example, if a coworker mentions that he took his kids to an Armenian Festival over the weekend, that might lead to you finding out that the person is of Armenian descent. That might not mean anything to you in the context of your jobs at the moment, but it might be significant down the line when that person has some take on an issue that differs from yours. If we never see difference, we tend to be clueless about why there may be dissent on issues where we believe there should be an "obvious" meeting of the minds.

## Happy Employees Are Better Employees

Satisfaction surveys have shown that employees who are happy at work make far more productive and loyal employees. Most people would agree that this makes sense. Anyone who has ever had to drag herself off to a job by force of willpower because of the dread of having to be at work would agree that this makes a lot of sense. However, most people would also agree that defining happiness at work is difficult.

One thing that I know creates unhappiness at work is feeling chronically misunderstood or out of sync. And wouldn't you be unhappy at work if you felt marginalized by others?

Many times, people are completely unaware of how they may contribute to an environment that marginalizes others. Everyone does it. No group or individual is immune from this behavior, which often manifests itself as a stray comment here or there or just outright ignoring any reflection of difference that butts against the edges of some particular norm. Sometimes, it's a barely perceptible way you treat someone different, but it's there and the person on the receiving end definitely feels it.

The purpose of diversity isn't to pass out candy and fly balloons in support of every group or articulated difference represented in the workplace. But it is to make people comfortable in the workplace. It is unrealistic to think that people can thrive in a work environment where there is tension or sometimes an overt lack of acceptance of the ways in which they define themselves. And often, these tensions and frustrations come in innocent conversations about news and pop culture events, through work gossip, or through the sharing of personal information over watercoolers or at company retreats and parties. We need to be aware of how important these personal interactions are in keeping workers happy and in sync with the people they work with.

## Teamwork Is Graded

A big criticism about diversity is that it strays too much from the "real" work of doing whatever job you're paid to do. Yet diversity is an important part of getting the job done.

Whether you sweep the company's floors or sign the paychecks of the people who sweep the floors, whether you're a teacher or a preacher, a police officer or an assembly-line worker, you probably have an annual performance evaluation of some kind. Rarely is there a true performance evaluation that fails to address your skills as a team player or your skills in dealing effectively with the customers, clients, or public you serve. Employees, including managers and supervisors, are judged on their ability to get along with others, which also includes how well they manage others and how well they are managed by others.

Most companies would do themselves and their workers a favor if they dealt with diversity issues in particular, and personnel issues in general, as an integral aspect of teamwork and people skills. And it's not a matter of having only bland conversations about bland topics. Part of diversity—which is part of teamwork—is learning to communicate with others in a way that is respectful and that hones your instincts so that you know when you're about to wade into tricky waters. Also, it's about navigating the tricky waters when you inevitably get in them.

## No-Cost Extras

We all love to get a little extra goody thrown in for free when we buy something—extra flavoring in the latte for free, a side of toast and fruit with the bacon and eggs for free, an extra window treatment tossed in with the ones we've already paid for. That's what diversity is like when you're different from the majority and you're treated well on the receiving end. Those people may take the job for the paycheck, but they may stay with that employer for years because of the "no-cost extra" of having their differences treated with acceptance and respect—and not like a scarlet letter *A* stamped on foreheads.

Maybe it's taking the ten extra seconds to smile at a coworker walking with a cane as you let her go through the door ahead of you even when you're running late for a meeting. Maybe it's going to the extra trouble of making sure that you are correctly pronouncing the name of your cubicle mate who is of Taiwanese descent. Maybe it's asking a coworker if a joke you told in the car on the way to a company luncheon offended her and then apologizing when she says it did.

In organizations, considerations of how you conduct yourself regarding diversity should be considered as important a part of your job as coming to work with good hygiene, speaking politely to people who speak politely to you, or smiling at the mail person or the janitor whom you pass in the hall. (You do find those considerations important, right?) Because if you find basic civility in the workplace a strain, exercising good diversity skills will be like aiming for a Ph.D. when you're working with a seventh-grade education.

## What You Take Away

On the flip side, sometimes it's about what you do not do at work that can contribute to the happiness factor of the people around you. You should, for example, make sure that you are not talking loudly about your personal views on abortion, saving conversations about religious dogma for some place other than the company lunchroom, not asking a coworker whom you never talk to some burning question about "what 'your' people think about …," and not using conversations about something on television or in the movies or in a book as a substitute for the bigger comments you want to make about a group of people.

Sometimes it's the things you choose not to do in the workplace that best pave the way toward helping to create a work environment where people are happier, functioning at their best, and thus keeping the company and the country rolling along so that everyone wins. One fewer off-color joke said at work probably represents at least a few hundred thousand dollars in lawsuits that will never have to be filed and a dozen or so fewer employees who are unnecessarily offended. As an employment lawyer, I saw more than once how one stray comment snowballed into a life of its own because on closer investigation it turned out that the one comment was part of a larger problem.

## Keys to Breaking This Chapter's Code

■ Jumping to conclusions about others might have been a valid response to the differences of others that people encountered back in caveman days, but it is not valid in modern times.

■ Happy employees are better employees, and creating an environment that allows for difference creates a happier and more productive environment.

■ Providing a more respectful environment is a no-cost extra that every employee can help produce to create a diverse workforce. Every little bit counts.

## Diversity Exercise

The next time you go to a public place, imagine if you had to sit at a table by yourself. Then, one by one, look at the people around you and ask yourself your instinctive reaction to how you would feel if each person asked to share your table with you. Don't judge or mentally argue with yourself—just honestly ask yourself what gut reaction you would have. Later, ask yourself which people triggered a "gut no."

Recognizing that you have these "gut no" reactions to others (no matter how much you may try to justify a good reason) is the first step in recognizing that a "gut no" might also be triggered at work.

## Group Exercise

Give a group of employees fifteen to twenty minutes to individually invent an employee evaluation form, coming up with five categories to judge employees on. Collect the forms and read them out loud, talking about the ways the lists of criteria are similar and different. Also, discuss if there are any ways that certain criteria could be unfair to people. For example, if someone has the criteria "has the ability to socialize easily with the entire department," talk about how that would unfairly evaluate someone who was an introvert or doesn't mingle with coworkers.

## Notes

1.   Wayne Lewis, "Escaping the Inner Caveman: USC College Psychology Experts Offer Perspectives on the Brain and Fear of Difference," April 1, 2007, http://college.usc.edu/news/stories/291/escaping-the-inner-caveman.

2.   Ibid.

# CHAPTER EIGHT

# Do White Guys Even Have to Worry About Diversity Since They Don't Have Any?

*Dear Diversity Diva:*

*I understand what you're saying. I buy what you're selling. I'm even singing in your Amen Choir. But I'm a straight white guy, so I don't have any diversity. That's right, isn't it?*

*Signed,*
*White Border on the Rainbow*

## White Men Can Jump

It has almost become a national gag how white men in America—straight ones with no disabilities—feel that they are becoming extinct. Even if all white men don't feel this way, the media often tries to make them feel as if they should.

It truly is one of the biggest misconceptions of diversity in the workplace. In part, it has been perpetuated by how corporate America has treated diversity in the workplace as a marginalized function of the bottom line. This was particularly so in the 1970s and 1980s, when the beneficiaries of the civil rights movement first entered the workforce with "good" management jobs ("good" being a respectable office job that required nice clothes and provided decent pay and benefits).

Oftentimes, those jobs were in the human resources department. In most companies across the United States, even in recent years, if you see only one vice president of color or one woman vice president, that person is often the vice president of HR. (Please understand that while I believe HR is one of the most integral components of a well-run company, most employees tend to view it as very far away from the company bottom line.)

Companies have realized in recent years that diversity has to include everyone in the workforce—including white men—with two trends showing evidence of that. The more prevalent trend is to add the word "inclusion" to the name of many diversity departments, programs, or titles. The symbolism of adding the word "inclusion" is to make sure that when the department or program addresses "diversity and inclusion" issues, it is sending the signal that no one is left out.

I think that symbolism is important and that word choices are critical to making a statement, but word choice can also obscure. Adding the word "inclusion," for example, furthers the notion that white men aren't normally part of diversity and therefore have to be specifically invited in.

Being included is always a good thing, but it's not always exclusion if you weren't personally and pointedly included in the first place. Granted, sometimes the distinction is murky. It's like my theory of lunch invitations.

If I invite my friend Anna to lunch, we're not excluding our mutual friend Elliot because we didn't proactively decide to invite (include) him to come along. We may want to talk about something that we know will bore him silly or something that is extremely personal and confidential between us. But for Elliot, who hears later that his two good friends went to lunch and didn't invite (include) him, it can feel the same as a deliberate exclusion. However, for Anna and me, it becomes a balancing act of deciding whom to include while also considering the feelings of those who will feel excluded if not invited.

The second and more slower moving trend that shows that companies realize that diversity has to include everyone is putting white men in charge of diversity programs or departments, to signal to the company and the community that diversity is important. In other words, it's so important that we put a white guy in charge to show that we're not marginalizing the issue. It would probably make a really good Diversity Brown Bag Luncheon to discuss if putting a white guy in charge for that reason still doesn't breed the same result of having workplace diversity viewed as a marginalized objective that needs to be headed by white males in the organization to gain legitimacy.

## Is Separate Ever Equal?

Separate as equal is a concept made well known by the famous 1954 Supreme Court decision *Brown v. Board of Education of Topeka,* which declared that separate educational facilities for different races were not equal, thus making segregation in public schools illegal.

One of the reasons why this concept can be a troubling topic to dissect, even in the context of workplace diversity, is because whites in general and white men specifically can feel as if they don't have the same leeway to openly express their heritage. Whites and especially white men, for example, may feel slighted because colleges have black and Hispanic and Asian and Native American student unions. The whites' cry is often, "If there was a white student union, there would be an uproar." From a purely linear standpoint, that position makes sense.

People get parallel understandings. If *black,* then there must be *white.* If *female,* then there must be *male.* If *gay,* then there must be *straight.* Groups, however, that have dealt with historical, systematic discrimination over a long period of time—where institutions have power and authority, or sometimes just official recognition—have created corresponding organizations to address equalizing gaps.

For example, the National Association of Women Lawyers doesn't exist to promote the idea that there is a boys' bar and a girls' bar. All lawyers may be created equal, but in a profession where men have decades of a head start in obtaining partnerships in law firms, being appointed to the bench, and obtaining other leadership roles in the legal profession, women's legal associations work to obtain fellowship and to create programming to make sure that women are closing the gap and becoming more adequately and fully represented in today's legal field. Whether through creating scholarships or providing mentorship programs, continuing legal education courses, and other initiatives that expose women to underrepresented areas of law, the purpose isn't to be anti-male. It's to be pro-opportunity for women.

Any profession or professional organization that targets a special segment of that field on the basis of a diversity difference has that purpose as the reason for its existence. There aren't many absolutes in the diversity field, but that would be one of them. While studies show that in education, boys are falling behind in terms of test scores and success, the numbers in the workplace arena still require historically disadvantaged groups to play "catch up" and address the different issues that come up for them in the workplace.

Trust me when I say that as someone who has been a member of various professional organizations catering to the interests of women and people of color for the past twenty-plus years, men and whites would probably have their feelings hurt at just how little time is spent talking about them, let alone bashing them. But that's not the point. Some whites and men are concerned that the organizations are meeting so that members will get a "leg up," which creates a vicious cycle of everyone worrying that some other group is getting an advantage over the group they are in.

## Win-Win for All

One of the arguments made against affirmative action is that it is unfair, and minorities are treated as if they are "less than" and thus get jobs they don't deserve. Hence, when talking about minorities at work, people are fond of acting as if the word "qualified" has to naturally go before the word "minorities," as in "We're looking to recruit more qualified minorities to the workforce," or "Several of our recent hires are qualified minorities whom we met at local job fairs." But I wonder if most white males have ever given thought to the presumption of competence that greets them at the workplace door whether they have earned it or not. Some may think that this is no longer the case, and I wholeheartedly agree that younger people entering today's workforce are less likely to hold that view than those most established in the workforce, but I feel that is still a very strong bias, based on studies and my various experiences dealing with workplace diversity and workplace discrimination.

If the point is that no person, regardless of race or gender or any other non–work-related factor, should get a job or job benefit unless it is based on merit, then there needs to be an equal opportunity recognition that it's not just minorities who benefit from systems and programs and just plain lucky breaks.

One could argue that there are so many eyes watching when companies have an affirmative action program that the instances of companies hiring vastly under-qualified minorities is rare compared to the hiring of under-qualified whites. If anything, it appears to be a common practice to have minorities and/or women who have to be vastly over-qualified to "prove" their merit.

For example, I recently became acquainted with a company in the Midwest that has been lauded for years with awards and publicity for its outstanding diversity efforts. This is one of those companies that is frequently listed on the "Best Places to Work" lists for its industry. But in the company's most recent group of summer interns, only one individual out of more than twenty was a racial minority (and also a woman)—and she was also the only individual who had two Ivy League degrees, for both her undergraduate and postgraduate work. In other words, all the nonminorities came from local universities and schools that were far lower on the prestige meter than the two schools the lone "qualified" minority attended. Unfortunately, that phenomenon is not unique to that particular company or industry.

So, is the point that this company was racist/sexist in perpetuating a double standard? Not necessarily. My point is that having this discrepancy in background between its white interns and its sole minority female intern helps perpetuate the subconscious promotion of the idea that being white, or being a white male, is a credential in and of itself that minorities have to live up to in order to prove that they are indeed deserving and qualified.

## Power Position

Traditionally, in pretty much every culture since the beginning of time, race, color, and distinctions regarding those issues have been the primary markers of how people evaluate power and class. Still, even in the United States today, when we glance at people in certain situations, we let the visuals of race and gender determine our knee-jerk assessment of who and what we think they are. So, in many ways, it is completely understandable why white men feel as if their race and gender, especially in combination, make them "devoid" of diversity.

But other defining issues compose the measure of a man—yes, even a white man. The most obvious points of demarcations are white men who are gay or have some sexual orientation other than straight and white men who have physical disabilities that are obvious or widely known. Other distinctions that can cause pause in terms of differences are white men who aren't Christian and who openly express membership in a religious or spiritual practice that isn't mainstream and white men who are married to women outside their race, especially if they have children. There may also be white men who are married to particularly high-powered or rich and famous women. Other distinctions may be socioeconomic background, height, weight, and fame unrelated to their job.

In all the cases mentioned, these white men have perspectives that are unique and distinctive from those of all the other white men who on the surface look just like them.

## Social Change Changes Things for Everyone

Although the social changes that women and ethnic minorities have gone through are widely documented and discussed, these aren't isolated changes. Rather, they affect all of society. For example, more women working and having comparable jobs to men in the workplace (with a significant section of today's women making more money than their husbands), along with no significant decline in the number of people marrying and having babies, affects the overall role of men and how that changed role affects them in the workplace. In addition, there are new occurrences that are now more commonly seen in today's workplace, such as men leaving work early as a result of child-related activities, men taking vacation days to spend with their families, men adjusting their work schedules to drop off or pick up children from daycare, and men even taking paternity leave when their wife has given birth or the family has just adopted a child.

So while many would argue that the role of juggling parenthood with jobs still falls disproportionately on the heads of working mothers, that still doesn't negate the fact that being a man in the workplace isn't quite the same today as it was even as recently as twenty years ago.

Even the evolving laws have caught up to this notion. The Family and Medical Leave Act (FMLA), for example, doesn't address just the need for women to take time off for family and medical reasons the way the Pregnancy Discrimination Act primarily does. The FMLA makes no distinction between men and women when it comes to job protection as it relates to taking a leave from work because of family and medical issues—even new additions to the family.

## Backlash

With the increased attention to equalizing the rights of the disenfranchised in our society comes the inevitable backlash as the status quo stakes go up. A column I wrote that ran the day President Obama was inaugurated and sworn in as the first black president of the United States stated that his inauguration wasn't a sign that affirmative action was no longer necessary. Instead, his inauguration wasn't anything more than an isolated accomplishment by one man based on a lot of battles that went into paving the way, and the battle for many groups—particularly regarding diversity in the workplace—still rages on even as progress continues to be made.

Not one hour after the inauguration, I received a blistering e-mail from a white male reader that said he was sick of racism against white men not being addressed by anyone. In his mind, all he could see and hear was that—to paraphrase a column written by Professor Andrew Manis, a white male college professor from the South—white males had become "demoted to equality" with nonwhites.[1] The angry e-mail writer was in the position that many members of non-mainstream groups have been in—wondering if their fears of being marginalized and dismissed would be taken seriously.

Some don't think of it as backlash. Some think of it as a legitimate reaction to the dynamics of a changing America.

Changing dynamics are something that the whole world needs to adjust to. For example, in 2009, China surpassed Germany as the top exporter in the world. That's a real shift in power, with one nation topping another nation that has an entirely different historical and cultural lineage. That's an example of the shifts that we all are getting used to as dynamics and power shifts change both within the United States and throughout the world.

## Looking in the Mirror

"When I look at you, I see myself. If my eyes are unable to see you as my sister, it is because my own vision is blurred. And if that be so, then it is I who need you either because I do not understand who you are, my sister, or because I need you to help me understand who I am."

—LILLIAN P. BENBOW,
national president of Delta Sigma Theta from 1971 to 1975

Although this quote is from a woman who was the president of a black college sorority, the sentiment applies to all men and women when it comes to getting a grasp of why diversity should matter to white men and to all people.

It is easy to see why it is important to get along with other people. It's a little less easy to understand why you have to understand others. And for most people, it may not be clear at all how understanding and accepting other people helps you to understand yourself and to be understood by others. One of the reasons is because demographics change. For example, a twenty-five-year-old white man is always going to be a white male (sex change operations notwithstanding) for the duration of his work career. But as he ages, he won't always be the bright shining new penny in the workplace. At some point, he will be older, and eventually, he'll be among the oldest of the people he works with. And if he continues to be an employee who answers to others, he will see how differently the young white men or young white women or young people of all racial backgrounds are treated and perceived compared to him.

In addition to aging, some white men will develop illnesses or have injuries. Others will come out of the closet regarding their sexuality. Some will undergo religious evolution or adopt philosophies that go against the grain of others where they work. A man may become the lone divorced person in a sea of happily married men. Or he may marry a woman of a different race, class, or generation.

In other words, change happens, and while you may be in the majority or the power position at one point of your life, you may not be in that position in another place or another time. Therefore, the compassion you learn to acquire today, when you don't "need" to be understanding, is the same compassion that you will want demonstrated toward you in the future or toward the people you care about. And exercising compassion and exhibiting goodwill and understanding become habits that you can demonstrate during the course of your entire working life.

## Keys to Breaking This Chapter's Code

- White men sit at the diversity table with their own individual issues of diversity.

- Separate can be equal but only if the purpose is to be "pro" you instead of "con" someone else.

- Power shifts, so the understanding you have for others will one day spin its karmic wheel, and a group that is "down" will become "up" and vice versa.

## Diversity Exercise

If you honestly think you have no diversity, look at your city's local calendar and circle or write down five events that, in the course of your normal life, you would only be caught dead at. If you're a die-hard sports fan whose middle initials are ESPN and the only music you like is what they play when the players come out on the court, then circle the opera gala. If your idea of cutting-edge music is the Doobie Brothers after Michael McDonald left the group, write down the Lil Wayne concert coming up. It's amazing how clear it is to see diversity in imagining yourself in the places where you don't normally go.

## Group Exercise

As a manager, come up with four or five short but different scenarios tailored to your department or workplace, and develop two different ways that each situation could be handled that seem evenly reasonable. Have the group members physically divide themselves on which way they would handle each scenario. Don't let people get away with standing in the middle. Let their decisions prompt a discussion on the diversity of approach. Have the fact that in every scenario there were people on both sides of the line trigger a discussion on why they made their decisions. Discuss if there were any themes or patterns shown by which people took which approach.

## Note

1.    Andrew M. Manis, "When Are WE Going to Get Over It," editorial in *Macon* (GA) *Telegraph*, January 2009.

# CHAPTER NINE

# If I'm a Member of a Minority Group or Have a Best Friend or Spouse Who Is, Then I'm Covered on Diversity, Aren't I?

*Dear Diversity Diva:*

*I understand how important all this diversity stuff is, but really, my company doesn't need to keep sending me to these diversity workshops. After all, I'm Jewish and my closest friend on the church softball team has a Jamaican mother and a Chinese father. I've learned tons from her so now I'm sensitive to others. I'm sure you agree, right?*

*Signed,*
*Kissin' Cousin to Diversity*

## Some of My Best Friends Are Black

As an employment defense attorney, a significant aspect of my job involved interviewing witnesses to prepare for a case. When interviewing individuals who have been accused of discriminating against a coworker or a subordinate, I experienced a ridiculously common occurrence when they said that they couldn't be prejudiced because their spouse/girlfriend /boyfriend /best friend/drinking buddy/favorite neighbor/youngest grandson's baby's mama is a fill-in-the-blank minority group member. Somehow, people who aren't members of a minority group believe in their hearts that close kinship with someone who is a minority group member grants them dispensation from ever being considered prejudiced or having ever discriminated against another.

It's true that there are people who look at the world a little more gently and with more compassionate understanding than their own life circumstances might prepare them for. It's true that some people truly love or befriend others and have increased sensitivities to the lives of others who are different. But even when that is the case, it doesn't necessarily mean that the sensitivity extends past, say, the person you care about or past the group that your loved one belongs to.

Also, just because you keep saying it doesn't mean it's true. An example from the news came in 2009, when Keith Bardwell—a justice of the peace in Louisiana—openly admitted to refusing to issue marriage licenses to interracial couples despite not having the legal right to make that decision. (He later resigned after the controversy this sparked.) "I'm not a racist. . . ," he said. "I have piles and piles of black friends. They come to my home, I marry them, they use my bathroom. I treat them just like everyone else."

## Bigotry Does Discriminate

As I said earlier in this book, some of the most bigoted statements I've ever heard come out of the mouths of people who are themselves in a traditionally disadvantaged group. What can be a more difficult dynamic to understand is when either bigoted or negative words come out of the mouths of people within the same group.

The most obvious example is the use of the "n" word in song or conversation by blacks to other blacks. Although some might argue that the use of the word is always wrong, regardless of who says it, I personally am not in that camp.

Complex reasons exist for why groups refer to themselves by words that would be ridiculously offensive if used by someone outside the group. It's just like how family can talk negatively about family members but be a united front to "outsiders." The same dynamic is at play when the family is a group. Women can call themselves "bitches" or "heifas" in jest. Gays can come up with slogans like "We're here, we're queer, get used to it." Europeans can poke fun at their intracontinental rivalries, but an "ugly American" better not get in the mix.

I once conducted diversity training for a municipality. One exercise involved choosing to sit next to one of a variety of different kinds of people. One of the options was sitting next to a coworker who was a member of the gay, lesbian, bisexual, or transgender community. The open hostility expressed about having to sit near a person who was not straight was almost always uttered by someone black or Hispanic.

One Hispanic woman said, "I wouldn't know what to say to them. What we would have in common?" When one of the other trainers asked her how she would feel if someone of a different race had that same reaction to having to sit near her, even though the trainer approached the point with a soft touch, the woman immediately got very defensive and upset that she wasn't "allowed" to have her opinion.

Others in the room from all groups may have had the same sentiments, but time and time again, I saw that the members of racial minority groups were most comfortable with verbalizing their distaste and aversion, almost as if their own status as a minority gave them the right to do so. And whenever it was pointed out that they would feel bad or hurt if a white coworker or a white stranger echoed the same sentiments about sitting next to a person of their race, they would be offended, hurt, and angry. Usually, when such a dichotomy was pointed out, it fueled a more intense settling in of the position and increased their validation of their right to feel that way.

## How Do You Get People to See That They Are Not Seeing?

Personally, I've found that people who have associations with minority group members are among the toughest nuts to crack on diversity issues. I've observed that this is because they take pride in having traveled the road of not being as divisive or prejudiced as some from their background or family are. This is true of people from different backgrounds, ranging from suburban to rural to different parts of the country to differences in socioeconomic status.

For example, a woman who has been raised by a very prejudiced family but who grows up to marry a man of Iranian descent is going to be particularly irate if a coworker accuses her of being discriminatory in her actions toward Hispanic subordinates. But the retort of "I'm married to an Iranian so I can't be racist" doesn't address the issue.

Let's dismiss the fallacy of that statement one piece at a time. First of all, whether you're racist or not racist is irrelevant to whether you've discriminated against a specific person. It is no more relevant than whether people who are kind to their own children are kind to stray animals. Being racist or not racist is not the law's business—it's a personal conclusion and one that does not determine whether you've discriminated against another.

But for the sake of argument, let's just act as if it is relevant that you're not racist. Then, at best, the proof that you're married to an Iranian would just be "evidence" that you're not a racist when it comes to Iranians.

The knowledge of, positive exposure to, and understanding about one group of people can make an about-turn to hate or distaste and negative judgments where a whole other group is concerned.

There are probably extraordinary people who have walked this Earth who bear no ill will or hold no negative misunderstandings about any group of people. Maybe Nelson Mandela or Mother Teresa in her lifetime. Maybe. But most of us don't fit that bill. Most of us are open-minded and knowledgeable about certain kinds of people, possibly because of how we were raised or the people we've met along the way, but we can still be completely oblivious to some groups and completely hostile to other groups.

One of my favorite quotes from a speech I attended is where Dr. Cornel West, a writer, speaker, and professor at Princeton University, said "Justice is what love looks like in public." For me, that defines why I think diversity is one of a company or organization's highest priorities. In the workplace, the issue is more appropriately one of fairness rather than justice, but the principle remains the same. If people in the workplace don't feel as if fairness is in play, then every decision, every job change, every hiring, firing, promotion, or so much as a change in the brand of napkins provided in the cafeteria becomes tainted.

Part of fairness involves people who are minority group members remembering that their differences don't give them any license to marginalize the differences of others. When that happens, they are given less credibility when they say they have received unfair treatment.

An example comes to mind of a local controversy where I live. It involved a dress code policy at a downtown entertainment district operated by a private company. Many people in the community interpreted the dress code as racist because it appeared to target the clothing styles identified with young black and Hispanic males. When someone from the communications department of another organization wrote an e-mail criticizing the policy as "typical of the greedy Jewish owners," he set off a firestorm. This ended up being an unfortunate example of how any legitimate point the person had to make about one group's so-called racist behavior or decisions becomes negated by the offended party's own racist words.

Does that mean that any individual member of a group can forever dismantle the legitimate issues that the group faces? No, not even close. But it does weaken any empathy that anyone will have for the reaction of that individual to the harm that he or she speaks of. Also, it diminishes the ability to understand why something is offensive if the offended is running around offending. Get it?

In the example of the dress code policy, for example, right-minded people who aim to be fair can come to very different conclusions regarding whether a policy is discriminatory or not. Some may say that excluding people who wear baggy pants is targeted at young African-American males, while others may find it to be an objective and completely valid exclusion that has no basis in race.

However, for people sitting on the fence, unsure about how they feel about the issue, hearing that a black writer made a patently racist comment about Jews owning the establishment might be enough to help them decide on the basis of that unfortunate comment. You can't fight fire with fire, and you can't melt bigotry away with bigotry.

## Political Groupthink

On a larger political scale, the issue of competing bigotries became quite vocal in 2008 in California. The gay, lesbian, bisexual, and transgender (GLBT) community threw its collective support behind the election of Barack Obama, the first black presidential nominee in a major U.S. party, then got upset when a large number of black voters supported a proposition on the ballot against gay marriage. Some viewed this as a classic "tit for tat" situation in which one group of disenfranchised people should have supported the agenda of another group of disenfranchised people.

The situation in California was complicated. Many of the blacks who voted there weren't conscious and deliberate participants in the "deal" the GLBT leaders felt was at stake. The essence of the GLBT leaders' point, at its best, was about minority group solidarity. But groups are not interchangeable, and thus, understanding and support for their respective issues can never be. In this example, the GLBT members and the black groups also had another special interest group to consider: certain Christian segments who were firmly against gay marriage.

Therefore, since everyone is a member of several groups with complementary and competing interests, voting often turns on how people choose to meld the multiple alliances they align with. That left California, and other states, with a number of blacks who found closer allegiance with the interest of Christians than with the GLBT community on the issue of gay marriage.

## *Stuff That White People Like* or Any Chris Rock Joke

While I was shopping at a national chain bookstore's table of recommended books, I came across a hilarious (to me) book called *Stuff That White People Like,* written by a white male named Christian Lander. It was a parody listing the things that white culture is a big fan of. One of the items listed was black people, as in saying that one is familiar with the latest black author or entertainer or saying that one has a black friend for no other reason than that it sounds cool. White people also like things that make them feel culturally hip.

Although the book is just a white guy poking fun at white people, as with all really good comedy, it makes profound underlying points—even when it gets really raw and makes you uncomfortable. (Comedian Chris Rock is one of the best examples of this.) The most profound point is about how the majority culture (in this case, white Americans) likes to have enough knowledge and exposure to that which is different to feel "hip," but this does not translate to understanding and sensitivity to the history and current circumstances the different groups experience. Confusing exposure to another culture with deep understanding of that culture can come off as paternalistic at worst, benignly insensitive at best.

Comedy—in the appropriate context, which oftentimes is *not* at work—can sometimes be the best and truest way to wrap your arms around complex and controversial issues. That's one of the reasons why *Saturday Night Live* and Comedy Central provide as good a read on understanding current events and diversity issues as the nightly news programs and CNN do.

## Keys to Breaking This Chapter's Code

- Close kinship with others who are different from you doesn't make you immune from misunderstanding the issues that concern and involve them.

- Being sensitive to and exposed to one group that is different from you doesn't mean that you have the first clue about another group that is different from you.

- Your membership in an underrepresented group doesn't give you free range to be openly offensive about another group.

## Diversity Exercise

Think about things that you are very good at—if not good, at least extremely familiar with doing repeatedly. Name seven things. Maybe the list includes baking a 7-Up cake or bowling a perfect game or braiding your daughter's hair in perfect rows.

Now think about what it would be like to explain to someone on the phone exactly how to do one of those things as well as you do it.

It's hard to give experience by proxy, isn't it?

# CHAPTER TEN

# How Do I Figure Out How to Hear the Differences Around Me?

*Dear Diversity Diva:*

*This is just too hard! I've got to come to work and do my job well, worry about the people around me not screwing up their jobs, kiss up to my boss, not tick off the people whom I boss, and now you're expecting me to "get" the differences of all the people around me too? It's just too hard! Where am I even supposed to begin?*

*Signed,*
*Exhausted Before I've Even Started*

## Diversity Is as Diversity Does

It can be difficult knowing how to jump in with both feet where diversity is concerned. It's so much easier sticking to the people who think like you, reason like you, vote like you, and hold dear to their hearts the same values that you do in the same order as you. You can especially wrap a comfortable blanket around yourself if the people look like you and have moved through their lives having the same kinds of experiences as you. It's so much easier to live that way, isn't it?

But it really isn't that hard to bridge the gap, exposing yourself to knowing about how others live and how they think. It's sometimes just a simple matter of listening and following up with an open, sincere question. Sure, it could be that your question offends, but it's more likely that if you asked the question with an open mind and heart, you'll get a response that reveals a little more. Then you and the other person both learn and grow from the encounter.

## Not a Friendship Factory

In every workplace in America, you find at least one person, if not many, who proclaims, "I'm not here to make friends. I'm just here to do my job." I have one friend of several years who has always had that philosophy. She is a professional woman with a couple of degrees on her résumé. She's friendly as can be, and yet she doesn't believe in making friends at work. She rarely walks away from a job with a close friend she made in the workplace, although she does have those kind of friendships in her life.

She has also had more than a dozen jobs in the past fifteen years. While she's never been fired from any of the jobs, at some point she leaves for a better opportunity or because she's bored or because something just seems off, and the cure for what ails her is a new job.

Over the years, what I think is off is that she never really connects with any of her jobs. One of the ways to connect is by actually feeling connected to other people—other people who can key you in on the lay of the land, who tell you what you need to know, who sometimes just give you a purpose for going to work because the job itself provides a paycheck but not a lot of purpose.

There are some people who are truly just antisocial. But my friend isn't one of them. Yet in making her work life the one area of her world where she's not expressing a key part of herself, she sets herself up to start looking for an exit sign barely five minutes after she's gotten through the entry door.

Again, it may seem like I'm saying that there is something wrong with the philosophy of not making friends at work. In certain specific situations and peculiar workplaces, it may even be a smart approach to have. But camaraderie is the oil that keeps the engine of most workplaces running. And even when people stick to just talking about work, there is always an undercurrent of personality, personal viewpoint, and nuances housed in cultural context that overshadows even the mildest interactions at work.

FRED: Morning, Jessica.

JESSICA: Good morning, Fred.

FRED: Could you please pass me the Anderson file?

JESSICA: Here you go.

FRED: Thank you.

That's a simple exchange. Very factual. Devoid of fleshiness or interpretation. Very work-directed and work-oriented. Also, except for the rare coworkers, an amazingly unrealistic reflection of any workplace in America. People don't talk this way. Even during a recent midair tragedy, the air traffic controller was criticized for alleged spending time talking on the phone about a dead cat found on the runway instead of directing air traffic the way he was supposed to. Real people interact. That's why reality TV is still raging in popularity.

Therefore, the exchange between Fred and Jessica is far more likely to go something like this:

FRED: Hey, Jessica. What's shaking? How was your weekend?

JESSICA: Good, really good. Too short as usual. How was yours?

FRED: Same. The wife and I rented *The Da Vinci Code* since we didn't see it when it first came out. Her pick, so I didn't know too much about it. Good little plot but not very realistic. Hey, could you hand me the Anderson file?

JESSICA: What do you mean it wasn't realistic? I loved that movie. Thought it was fascinating, particularly the part about Jesus and Mary's real relationship.

FRED: Real relationship? C'mon, that movie and that book is a bunch of crap. It's just a story, and anyone who believes that really happened needs to read *the* book about Jesus.

JESSICA (practically throwing the file at Fred): Here you go.

FRED: Thanks. See you and the gang at lunch.

Now *that* is more like it. One quick conversation about something completely unimportant, plump with meaning, innuendo, and viewpoint. Depending on how many other conversations Fred and Jessica have had, this conversation can either enhance their working relationship or diminish it.

In some rare cases, an exchange like this could have a neutral effect on their working relationship, but that would most likely be because they had talked enough in the past to have pretty well established their opinions about each other. Even in those cases, however, some of those conversations will be held in the earshot of others, which means that the conversations get repeated to others who then form their own opinions, and so on and so on.

Unfortunately, in the workplace and in work-related situations, opinions and judgments tend to be very fixed when change is forced or sought after directly. Recently, when I was giving a speech on diversity to a group of people in an industry not applauded for rapid change, the looks on the faces of the people in the audience were the same from the beginning of the speech to the end with only a couple of exceptions. The faces that were fixed, immobile, and resistant when I began speaking remained fixed, immobile, and resistant when I left. The faces that were open, engaged, and interested when I started speaking remained open, engaged, and interested. There was mental movement on the subject of diversity by a few people. But I know the real shift happens back at the workplace, when they have a passing conversation with a coworker that they would not have had before. Likewise, the real shift happens if they have the ability to hear the conversation a little differently than they would have before.

## When the Student Is Ready, the Teacher Will Appear

One of the reasons why I feel bad when I leave a diversity workshop and have seen more resistant faces than engaged ones is because I know that no matter how profound or brilliant I may have mentally patted myself on the back for being, to the people closed to what I'm saying, anything coming out of my mouth sounded only like preaching. Deep down, even people who go to a place of worship don't really want to be preached at—especially about something they don't think they are getting wrong to begin with. They want their minister or rabbi or priest or spiritual leader to teach them something—to reveal something they don't know because it seems hidden or to remind them of what they already knew, so they can obtain their individual stroke of spiritual or religious enlightenment.

Part of being truly taught, however, comes from the person wanting and willing to be taught. As the saying goes, "When the student is ready, the teacher will appear." That's what diversity in the workplace can be about—

being open to the differences that other people experience and the different ways they show up in the workplace. Unfortunately, you can't make other people ready. You can model behavior that allows someone to see the advantages of being open rather than closed to differences. But even with that, the person has to decide to follow your lead.

"Manners are a sensitive awareness of the feelings of others. If you have that awareness, you have good manners, no matter what fork you use," said Emily Post on the subject of modern etiquette. That is pretty much what diversity in the workplace requires: an ongoing, conscious desire to have a sensitive awareness to the people you work with. Listen to what the people around you say, how they talk, how they use language, what they talk about, and whom they talk to.

Also, keep awareness up of whom the people around you do not talk to, what conversations they have with some but not with others, how their tone and intonations and body language change with some people from how they are with others. In observing other people—even those who appear to be exactly like you in surface ways—you learn how to treat others. This is especially important when circumstances at work leave you needing to understand how your differences with other people cause you to clash over those differences, and especially if others feel as if they are being treated poorly or unfairly.

Spiritual teacher Michael Bernard Beckwith says it best when he writes that sympathy is when you ask how someone is feeling. Empathy is feeling the way someone else is feeling, while compassion is actually understanding why someone feels the way she does and then seeking the opportunity to help her walk her path.[1]

Also, it's not always the people who fail to share some same group membership with you who lack sympathy or empathy or compassion. It may be people in a group you are in who are trying to actively block your progress in understanding others. Your "own" people can be anchors wrapped around your legs in the sea of progress and success.

## Compassion and Integrity

That is what diversity in the workplace really requires—compassion. Not you seeking to differentiate yourself from every person who crosses your path on any given day, and certainly not wrapping yourself in the superiority blanket where you reach down to understand the plight of others.

In addition, while compassion is what generates how you choose to see others, integrity is the external way you act that practice out. Is your behavior in congruence with the compassion you believe you have toward others?

For example, say a coworker comes to work complaining about how difficult it is as a divorced parent to manage four school-age children. He is frazzled about getting his workday started. Compassion will be the voice that really feels bad for his situation, maybe even says how bad you feel about his situation when you're having lunch with other buddies at lunch. But it's integrity that causes you to offer concrete suggestions about how your coworker could improve his morning routine once he gets to work, while still maintaining the compassion. Granted, it may be that your coworker didn't ask for your advice. But between the choice of talking behind his back and offering suggestions when he comes to you to vent, most of the time, the suggestions are the better way to go unless you want to just kindly tell him not to vent to you at all.

I have a dear friend whom I met in the workplace. For years, she has had the ongoing refrain of "Why do people talk to you?" She asks this because I'm famous for having people I worked with coming back to me for advice even when my advice can be pretty brutal—honest and well meaning, but not pretty. I always say that when I start lying or acting without integrity when I give advice (which is usually telling them something they already know themselves), then people will stop seeking out my opinion.

Sometimes, integrity is the opposite of talking. It's keeping your mouth shut about a coworker's situation—keeping judgment on her life to yourself and not providing fodder for the gossip and putdowns of others.

Sometimes diversity is about understanding and knowing, and sometimes it's about just keeping silent as you work through what you have yet to understand or know in order to better understand and work with others.

## Keys to Breaking This Chapter's Code

- Building relationships at work lays a strong foundation for understanding diversity.

- Even when you don't consider friendships at work to be critical, that doesn't mean your interactions with others at work aren't laden with meaning and subtext.

- Compassion is caring about the feelings, viewpoints, and life circumstances of others. Integrity is acting upon that compassion.

## Diversity Exercise

If you are someone who never eats lunch away from your desk, ask a coworker to go to lunch with you sometime.

If you are someone who always eats with the same person or group of people, take a rain check and ask someone else to lunch one day. The person you pick doesn't have to be dramatically different from you in any way. The diversity is in your getting to know someone different, which makes it easier for you when you're ready to pick someone dramatically different from you in a way you find significant.

## Group Exercise

Bring in your town or city's local daily newspaper. One facilitator should randomly read headlines and the first few paragraphs of stories throughout the newspaper. Try to find a variety of articles involving a variety of people and/or events. For example, read a story about the tattoo explosion in the suburbs and a story about the Future Farmers of America convention coming to town. While this is happening, have another facilitator take notes on the group reactions to the different stories, as well as the body language of individual participants. When about half a dozen or so stories have been read, have the facilitator who took notes read out loud the various reactions, and let that trigger a discussion about how people react to differences even when they aren't aware of them and how reactions, even nonverbal ones, impact other people.

## Note

1.    Michael Bernard Beckwith, *Spiritual Liberation: Fulfilling Your Soul's Potential* (Hillsboro, OR: Atria Books/Beyond Words, 2009).

# CHAPTER ELEVEN

# How Do I Avoid Overstepping, Being Too Personal, or Creeping into Sexual Harassment Territory?

*Dear Diversity Diva:*

*So I'm really good friends with this woman at work. We go to lunch together every day, we take breaks together, and she really is the only person here I trust. Only the deal is, I'm a guy. I'm not hitting on her or anything, but am I doing something wrong that I'll get in trouble for some day?*

*Signed,*
*BFF with a Babe at Work*

## Statistics Tell the Story

As of 2008, women were 46.5 percent of the total workforce in the United States. That's practically half. So while some workplaces may be short on diversity when it comes to race, nontraditional sexual orientation, disability, and many others points of visible and not so visible difference, if you work and throw a rock, you will almost certainly hit someone of the opposite sex.

Because so many men and women work together, there is a huge issue of how they can work better together without triggering sexual harassment complaints. I'm devoting a chapter to it because this entire book advises you to ask questions, talk to others, explore differences, make yourself uncomfortable sometimes—generally, to put yourself in the position of getting to know others so that you can appreciate, respect, and successfully work beside the differences of others in cases where difference matters.

Therefore, because the interaction between men and women is so common, there need to be some general guidelines on how people can learn to interact with men and women without necessarily triggering fear of a sexual harassment complaint.

## Start with Definitions

Let's start off with the legal definition of sexual harassment so that we can take that off the plate and the chapter can address the overwhelming bulk of the way that men and women interact that does not fall under the rubric of harassment.

Generally speaking, in the United States, there are two kinds of sexual harassment: *quid pro quo* and *hostile work environment*. (In the United States, sexual harassment is a civil matter. In France sexual harassment is defined differently and the accused can be charged with a criminal offense.) Quid pro quo means "this for that." This type of sexual harassment is a direct request for sexual favors in exchange for job benefits or continued employment.

An example of quid pro quo is Lila, a manager, threatening to fire Enrique if Enrique doesn't sleep with her. And for those who think this example is just a case of me being cute or diverse by making the harasser a woman and the person harassed a man, that's not the case. In fiscal year 2008, men filed 15.9 percent of the sexual harassment claims received by the EEOC.

The other kind of harassment is hostile work environment. (This standard also applies to harassment on the basis of race, color, national origin, religion, age, and disability.) In this type of sexual harassment, behavior or speech can be severe or pervasive enough on the basis of sex to create an abusive work environment for an employee that interferes with his or her work.

For example, Franklin likes to bring magazines with scantily clad women on the cover to work and leave them lying around on his desk. He does this daily, and it offends the heck out of Katherine, who has the desk next to him. Combined with the crude comments about women that Franklin frequently makes, Katherine has the basis for bringing a sexual harassment complaint regarding Franklin under the legal theory of hostile work environment on the basis of sex.

## Assumptions About Male-Female Friendships

Sociologists, life coaches, marital counselors, fundamentalist preachers, and by-the-book HR officials all have distinct and differing views on the subject of interaction between men and women in the workplace. As previously stated, women make up almost half the U.S. workforce, so men and women are always interacting. And any way you slice it, male-female relationships in the workplace can be complex and awkwardly complicated.

For example, in most workplaces where there is no significant strain of hostility toward openly gay employees, no one thinks twice about a work friendship between an openly gay male and a straight female. No matter how attractive or young or single either the man or the woman is, no one really thinks twice about it. There are rarely whispered conversations, nosy speculations, or puzzling vibes that management may feel it has to keep an eye on.

For some, those circumstances don't develop because of pure stereotype—the assumption that it's okay for a gay man and a straight woman to be friends because they have lots to talk about, an assumption based on watching too many sitcoms or plays where gay men are depicted as "one of the girls." But the real reason most people don't give it a second thought is because while the relationship (excuse me, friendship) is between two people of the opposite sex, it's not two people interested in each other for romantic relationship possibilities. That's why the key in this scenario is that the male is openly gay. In a situation where the man is not "out," there will likely be speculation, awkwardness, curiosity, and attracted attention. Even in situations where the buzz doesn't get back to those particular coworkers, the gossipy speculation and wondering and commentary can be an unnecessary, disruptive, harmful snag in the fabric of the department or company where these two people work.

## Sexual Tension Where There Is None

We live in a country obsessed with sex. Even the hard-down moralists and profoundly religious are obsessed with sex in their aversion to having the subject be such a big part of our society.

In our contemporary society, we have seen improbable, unlikely, and in some cases completely reprehensible things surrounding the issue of sex in the workplace. We observe sexual innuendo and subtext both where there is none and when there is way too much.

So, on the one hand, when we see a woman manager in her fifties befriending a young male college graduate, some may think that this is a cool example of mentoring, while others think "cougar on the prowl." The same thing happens when there is a nice, helpful, married man who becomes friendly with a female coworker who graduated from the same out-of-state university that he did. Some see nothing more than alumni bonding, while others see another married guy trying to get a little something on the side.

There is no category of male-female friendship where the possibility of something inappropriate or outright unlawful can be eliminated. That's because millions of people have seen the workplace serve as the backdrop for their sexual relationships, for where they meet their future (or former) spouses, for their extramarital affairs, or as where they know of others who have engaged in one of these multitude of possibilities.

When you add the nonconsensual male-female relationships that happen at work in the form of sexual harassment, the variety of ways that men and women can interact requires more than casual analysis.

## Awareness as the Appetizer

One of the first things that any man or woman needs to do when entering a new work environment or following the changing tide of an existing work environment is to observe. Do people frequently go out to lunch together? If so, are they mixed groups of men and women, or do the groups tend to bond by gender? How do people bond and communicate at work? Do they visit other people's offices or desks or cubicles or workstations, or do they do most of their bonding by e-mail or telephone? Do people who bond at work do so across department, work function, or status? For example, do managers go to lunch with subordinates for reasons other than work?

These aren't small considerations because understanding the norm of workplace bonding lets you know when you step outside the norm. This is especially true when you are developing a friendship at work with someone of the opposite sex, and you will receive heightened scrutiny if you step outside the norm.

For example, in a real estate company where people routinely eat lunch at their desks if they are not out on sales calls, it will attract attention if

Philippe and Yvonne go out to lunch by themselves two or three days a week. Most people won't jump to the conclusion that absolutely nothing but friendship is going on between them since their actions are so outside the norm of the work culture. While this doesn't mean harassment is taking place, the situation will spark gossip.

## No Such Thing as "Reverse" Harassment

Just like with the issue of discrimination, there is no such thing as "reverse" sexual harassment. With racial discrimination, for example, there is no such thing as reverse discrimination, where it's okay if a white person is discriminated against by a Hispanic, but it's a legitimate claim if the same behavior is directed at a Hispanic by a white person. Nope, harassment doesn't work that way either.

It's important to keep that in mind regarding friendships with members of the opposite sex. If you're a woman—more specifically, a woman with more rank than your male friend—in most cases, this will not be an issue. But as with all circumstances, there are exceptions when people go astray or do not calculate the ramifications. In some cases, depending on the sexual orientation of the people involved, these considerations don't necessarily have to involve the opposite sex.

## Exercise Good Judgment

Men and women can have successful friendships in the workplace. But they need to exercise good judgment. Here's an example of why that's important.

Sue was a mid-level manager at an organization with about a dozen departments. She and one of her subordinates, Dan, were good buddies going back to when they both started at the company at roughly the same time. Both were married. Sue and Dan's personal relationship never strayed from strictly platonic territory. However, they had a raw, bawdy, back-and-forth joking between them that was not appropriate for workplace e-mail and particularly not between a department manager and one of her subordinates. Worse, Sue had gotten in the habit of joking about how she would cut back on the amount of Dan's recommended raise at his next performance evaluation if he didn't start "putting out" after the department happy hours that took place on Friday afternoons.

Is Dan likely to sue the company for sexual harassment based on their e-mails? People have tried based on less, with the result that companies have had to pay significant amounts of money in confidential settlements.

My point isn't to comment on whether Dan would have a good or a weak legal case, since the legal concept of "welcomeness" (evidence to show that he doesn't mind the behavior he's now complaining of because he participated or "welcomed" the same behavior in the past) and other factual details would be significant issues to be dealt with. But I mention it to point out that in having opposite-sex friendships in the workplace, the respective genders of the employees won't matter if a complaint of sexual harassment is ever brought up.

As with all things involving diversity, awareness and exercise of good judgment go a long way toward having one of the enriching and harmless male-female friendships that contribute to a positive work environment.

## Keys to Breaking This Chapter's Code

■ Men and women work side-by-side in great numbers today. This is just a simple fact of life that's not going away, so male-female interactions in the workplace can't be completely avoided.

- Being aware of how others in your workplace interact—paying attention to your particular work culture—makes opposite-sex relationships easier to manage.

- Women have to be just as careful as men in making sure that they are not being inappropriate or giving the appearance of impropriety since they too can be on the receiving end of a sexual harassment complaint.

## Diversity Exercise

Do a scan of your workplace and examine how the men and women generally get along. Do people seem to have open, above-board friendships and friendly work relationships? Are there a lot of people who are in open relationships with others— in other words, people openly dating or even married to other people in the same organization? Or is this a workplace where there are a lot of covert relationships taking place—relationships that everyone knows and whispers about even though they're ostensibly secret? Or is your workplace a combination of the above?

The funny thing about this exercise is that it may be the most difficult exercise in this book to do if you aren't the type of person who has already observed this. If, however, you're someone who naturally observes these things, this will be a "duh" exercise.

# CHAPTER TWELVE

# Doesn't Understanding a Difference Mean That I'm Accepting Something That I Don't Necessarily Support?

*Dear Diversity Diva:*

*I'm sorry, but there's a point where, even as a manager, I'm just not going to accept certain kinds of people. They may have the legal right to do certain things, but I don't approve of it and don't believe that I should have to accept them. Don't I have the right to not like or even accept everyone?*

*Signed,*
*Rubbed Wrong by Having to Rub Elbows with Some*

—

## Acceptance Starts After Perception

In the November 2008 election between Barack Obama and John McCain, the United States elected its first black president. The country—even the half that didn't vote for the eventual winner—collectively patted itself on the back for undoing its ugly history with race.

Fast forward a mere eight months later, when another Ivy League–educated black man put the issue of race and the still wide divide squarely back in America's face. When Harvard professor Henry Louis "Skip" Gates got arrested at his house in what he cited as a case of racial profiling gone amuck, the controversy raged on and on, far past the one-day news cycle that would have been generated if a white professor who taught at a local state school had been arrested.

In conversation after conversation that I overheard and got drawn into, it became clearer than it ever was that perception completely shades and forms factual understanding. Almost every person of a racial minority I talked to, with varying degrees of passion, believed that Gates was treated differently than he would have been if he was white. The perception of most minorities was founded on a number of facts: personal experience with police officers and other authority figures, the anecdotal experiences of family and friends of the same racial background, statistics on racial profiling, historical background, and just plain old gut instinct based on an insistent hammering of the tensions between black males and the police in our society.

Many of the whites that I overheard or talked to, though, had a different perception of the same facts. The focus was more on the right of a police officer to investigate a reported potential crime, the correctness of the procedures, the ways that Gates responded to the police, and just a general view of this as an isolated issue rather than as the global, societal marking that it became.

The disconnect rolled into outright hostility when President Obama initially weighed in on the issue at a press conference by saying that the police acted "stupidly," making very apparent which perceptual take on the matter he assumed.

Same facts, different perception, with each position hardening based on where people chose to focus their attention. This is a classic example of how good, smart, right-thinking, fair-minded people can profoundly disagree on the facts. And when the facts require more than the mere tallying of numbers or some analysis that can be done with a set of test tubes and a clipboard, they don't always add up to the same conclusion.

## I Accept Except for What I Don't Accept

One of the quickest ways to shut down a heated conversation (or to make it heated if it wasn't hot before) is to say that your opinion about something is based on your religious beliefs.

When it comes to race or color, people generally know that openly stating your opposition to another group is a huge no-no. Racial prejudice as a socially endorsed, politically supported way of life is over. It's not, of course, that racial discrimination in the workplace is over. Far from it. It's not even to say that open racial hostility and discrimination don't exist. They do. It's just that issues of racial and gender-based discrimination are so frowned upon, and so subconscious when they do exist, that it defies logic for people to voice these opinions.

But discussions and opinions about religion are a whole different animal—a horse of a different, but accepted, color, so to speak.

Usually, the quickest way to keep someone from continuing a discussion about a disagreement is to state that your opinion is based on a religious belief. It's one of those conversation stoppers that leave the other person in the position of continuing to argue her position or appearing to attack your religion, which people generally do not want to do, especially if the religion being challenged is a mainstream religion.

MERI (trying to make small talk with her new coworker): So Don, what does your wife do for a living?

DON: She's a homemaker. She was a schoolteacher before we got married.

MERI: Does she miss teaching? Because I just read that the school district is looking to recruit former teachers to the district.

DON: Well, my wife and I don't believe, based on our religious teachings, that a wife needs to be out working in the world. That's my job as the head of the household.

Now Meri could attack, disagree, or just stand there staring at Don with her mouth hanging open because she finds his statement to be completely objectionable and sexist. But to attack that viewpoint—even if she has a similar religious background—would be to attack Don's belief system. And if you attempt to attack a belief system, you won't win, and you will certainly go way beyond the scope of the original disagreement.

Of course, religion is one of those topics that really needs to stay out of the workplace. This is especially so because religion can be the basis for a discrimination complaint under the EEOC.

For example, Don might have been better off keeping his thoughts to himself regarding why his wife didn't work outside the home. Although it was Meri who initiated small talk that was overly personal, Don would still have been better served to keep religion out of his workplace conversation with a person he didn't know. Don could have just left it at, "My wife's a homemaker now," and then turned the topic to something else. It would not have been rude for him to just not have answered the question at all and immediately turned the conversation to a work subject. Most people— with the exception of those raised in the woods by bears—know that an abrupt change of conversation after a personal question has been asked is a flashing signal that you have overstepped.

Realize that any awkwardness in Meri and Don's conversation isn't just on Don's head and on the answer he gave. In fact, their conversation provides a classic example of how people frequently broach topics in the workplace that veer into the acutely personal or marginally controversial, and then they get bent out of shape when they receive a response that offends them. Meri, in her attempt to make small talk with someone she doesn't know, would have been on safer ground sticking to things that were directly work-related or extremely safe. Sports and the weather are always gentle subjects. Recent news events can be dicey because even seemingly minor comments on events can be a short leap to conflicting opinions that can get real ugly real fast. The case of Professor Gates being arrested that I mentioned earlier in this chapter is an excellent example of a news event that may be too controversial to discuss at work.

Ultimately, every interaction between people in the workplace is about cause and effect. Therefore, if you cause the conversational path to go in a certain direction, you must be prepared for the effect of where you end up. Part of what this entails is knowing how to read your environment. Frankly, a lot of people don't know how to do this. This means that you have to understand which coworkers you should just discuss the weather with, to be aware of the timing at which you bring up certain things with other co-workers, and to know the people you can say anything to at any time as long as you mind where you are having the conversation.

## Tolerance and Acceptance

I'm probably going to make a statement that most diversity consultants wouldn't make, which is that while tolerance may be the gateway to acceptance, I think it's okay if people—on some issues or regarding some people—just aim for tolerance.

Acceptance is a form of embrace, an internal commitment to truly recognize the existence of certain people or cultures and the rightness of that existence. That may not be a dictionary or textbook definition, but when it comes to diversity, that's what it boils down to.

For example, when I say I accept that women can be high-ranking officers in the military, what I'm saying is that I find this a logical, obvious fact of life that doesn't contradict any thoughts I have about either women or the military. I'm accepting that it is right that women be allowed to hold those positions. It doesn't mean that my acceptance is about any individual women military leaders or even any reflection of my general feelings about the U.S. military.

Now some older (or not so much older) men who have served in the military and fought in one or more war zones, and who have been brought up in a certain way regarding the role of women in society generally, may never be in acceptance mode regarding women being in the military as soldiers, let alone accepting their "right" to achieve high rank. These men (and any women who may also hold that view) will never have acceptance of the existence of women as military leaders.

These people may have tolerance if they have to serve under those women as members of the active military, if they meet these women at military events, or even if they just read about them in the news.

Tolerance is below acceptance on the ideal scale of human interaction. When you tolerate something or someone, you're saying that you recognize the person or thing's existence, but you refuse to internally accept on any level that this is right. It's like the way you may feel about your next door neighbor who lets a week's worth of newspapers or circulars accumulate in his front yard when you are very particular about appearances. You tolerate that he has the right to do that, but you don't accept that it looks okay. In your tolerance, you probably won't bother saying anything to your neighbor about this issue because you recognize that it's his yard and his newspaper subscription, and he's not violating any city ordinances. But it still bugs the mess out of you, and it probably shows a little in your tiny, casual interactions—like waving over the fence or while getting in the car.

As easily as you can see this in your personal life, it becomes more pronounced in the workplace, where there can be more "forced" interactions with people or types of people you don't accept.

If people are deeply in touch with how they view others, they realize that there are far more people whom they tolerate but don't necessarily accept. Usually, the challenging categories aren't always the big-ticket diversity items that generally come to mind. For example, you may accept your black coworker until you realize that she's married to a white man.

Or you may accept your coworker who is in a wheelchair until you learn that he was on public assistance for years before he got his current job. Or you may accept the hard-working single woman with three young children to support until you learn that she's never been married to any of her children's fathers.

Obviously, we are all different in what we accept versus what we tolerate, which is why I chose to present the above examples. Each was chosen because there is always someone who holds that view. This underscores that we can't always accept the things we can tolerate. And for some individuals, when it comes to certain kinds of people or certain types of backgrounds, tolerance is the highest rung on the ladder they're going to climb.

## Diversity Is Just a Fancy Word for Differences

If our entire workplace language could shift like an episode of the *Twilight Zone* where you could do "find and replace" with a word, I'd love to see the mental shift that would take place if there were no more diversity departments, diversity workshops, diversity officers, or diversity initiatives. Instead, we could talk about differences and inclusion, a company's chief executive officer of difference, and a mandated company workshop called "Appreciating Workplace Differences and What It Means to Our Customers."

Think about how much less tense people would be if they had to spend a day in an annual workshop on differences. They might be annoyed. They would probably make fun of having to go there. But not as many people would get that angry, resentful, uncomfortable knot in their stomach or that low-grade irritation that occurs when they hear the words "Day-Long Diversity Workshop." What a difference a word makes.

One of the reasons that I know this is true is because I see the calmer, more amused way that people react to conversations about the ways people are different based on something less charged than "diversity." Take the common circumstance of birth order. That's an acceptable frame of reference regarding difference that people are familiar with and comfortable with. They can discuss this type of self-identification with ease and with rare defenselessness: "Oh, I'm a typical oldest child," or "That Jon, I can tell he's the baby of the family," or "Don't mind me, I'm used to being treated like the only child that I am."

People love classifications and love placing themselves in classifications, even while simultaneously denying the validity of it. Astrology is another great example. Most people in work or other professional settings pooh-pooh astrology, but studies show that most people know exactly what their own sun sign is. When there is no one around who they think will make fun of them, people say things like "Yep, I'm a control freak Virgo to a tee," or "When I pick up those astrology descriptions at the checkout line and read through them, I'm stunned at how much it sounds like me."

People like characterizing and classifications and systemic differences right up until we get to the issue of diversity, especially in the workplace. Suddenly, the defensive warning lights start flashing and the safety arm swiftly comes down. To a very real extent, that's understandable. Classifying someone as a stubborn Taurus or a loud-mouthed Sagittarius may find you catching an odd look, but it won't get you fired. Classifying someone as a PMS'ing woman, a fiery Latina, or a black guy with a scary attitude will almost surely put you in the direct line of unpleasant job consequences.

## Workspace, Not Workplace

The workplace really should more accurately be called the "workspace." The word *workplace* does a good job of identifying the physical, unchanging, concrete place where people go to do their jobs and collect their paychecks. The concept of workspace, however, describes the more fluid nature of what a job outside your home really requires.

In general, salespeople understand this best. Some salespeople have customers who come to them, which requires the salespeople to assess motivation, personality, budget, urgency, experience with the product, or other considerations of whether they will make a sale that day, sometimes with virtual strangers. Other kinds of salespeople have to visit their customers' sites, thus requiring the salespeople to add place, location, environment, other relationships, competitors, and other relevant factors that also determine whether this will be a single sale or an ongoing customer relationship.

Either way, making the sale is really about change. Those salespersons—at least the really successful ones—are comfortable with the concept of change, uncertainty, and movement when it comes to understanding and connecting with people who, depending on what they are selling, cross the longitude and latitude of humanity. They get that the workplace is really a workspace, where different kinds of people constantly move in and out of the space.

People working in more traditional, stationary jobs aren't always very comfortable with that concept. Just when they get used to having a woman boss, she leaves and they have to get used to a gay one. Just when they get adjusted to having a visually impaired coworker, she moves to a different department and they're sitting next to a woman of Islamic descent. Just as their department is really gelling together, an assertive personality type who has to question everything is added in.

In viewing where you work as a workspace instead of a workplace, you get comfortable with the one dependable thing in the dynamics of the workplace: change.

## Keys to Breaking This Chapter's Code

- There are few, if any, people who accept all differences equally.

- Sometimes, merely tolerating the differences of others is as close as some people will ever get to accepting others.

- The workplace is really a workspace where the only constant is change.

## Diversity Exercise

Think of something in your life that you are passionate about or an organization that you're actively involved in. Maybe it's your church or place of spiritual sustenance. Maybe it's your membership in the National Guard or your community involvement with Big Brothers Big Sisters. Maybe it's just your devout dedication and pride in being a parent or a caretaker for a beloved family member.

Now imagine how it would feel if every day you went to work, someone whom you work closely with made you feel as if there was something questionable, suspect, or just odd about your involvement or identification.

Crazy to even contemplate, isn't it?

# CHAPTER THIRTEEN

# How Can I Tell Whether My Company Is Really Diverse or If It's Just Saying It Is?

*Dear Diversity Diva:*

*I see that we have a few minorities in management in my company, which is a pretty big place. Also, the women here seem to be doing more than all right. And folks seem to get along well with everyone else. I guess that means my company is diverse, right?*

*Signed,*
*A Picture Is Worth at Least a Dozen Words*

## Comfort vs. Factual Conditions

When it comes to judging specific aspects of diversity, people almost always overestimate the number or percentage of "others." For example, let's say a married woman with children is a member of an organization that addresses the needs of local children. She thinks that there are "lots" of single parents in the organization. A look at the actual roster, however, indicates that out of more than eighty parents in the group, only seven head single-parent households. How does that misconception occur?

Oftentimes, innocently. Maybe the president of the organization is a single parent, so the assumption is that the leadership reflects membership. Or maybe the two people she sat near at a recent meeting are in that category, so she assumed there must be a large number.

Sometimes it's just the fact that people are incredibly self-absorbed, so they don't stop to assess diversity in regard to some aspect of a group as long as they feel comfortable. Therefore, if you see even one person who is "different" but you still feel comfortable, then you may label the entire group or department or company as "diverse" without really having to think about it.

## In Search of Camelot's Work Staff

To make things interesting, I decided to go in search of my idea of the perfect workplace when it comes to diversity.

### Size Matters

First, the place had to be big, or at least not small—about 800 to 1,000 employees all working in the same building. I picked that number because of the obvious reason: the more people, the more chances that differences show up. For example, if you have a business of, say, just fifty to sixty people, the number of people who come from a variety of backgrounds is greatly reduced.

In general, people tend to hire people whom they relate to in some way, and the fewer the bodies working for an organization, the easier it is to develop a "baseline" of what is considered normal. For example, I know of a medium-size law firm in St. Louis, Missouri, that at one point in the 1990s had eighty lawyers who were all graduates of Ivy League schools. Do you know how much conscious filtering, let along unconscious filtering, a law firm in Missouri has to go through to not have one graduate of a Missouri law school? So my perfect diversity organization has to be big.

## Working in One Building

My requirement that all the employees work out of one building is because it is easy to look like you have diversity on paper if you have, for example, the bulk of your Hispanic employees in your Florida and Texas offices, a large number of the African-American employees in your Atlanta and Detroit offices, and a large number of your Asian employees in your California offices. Meanwhile, if your main office is in the Midwest, there is no discernible racial diversity to be found outside of the support staff.

Even outside of racial diversity, with a business spread out in different offices—for purposes of the perfect diversity workplace—it's easier to have different standards of diversity because of the hiring practices of one office versus another. One office, for example, can have a manager who is completely open to hiring the physically disabled but shuts down when it comes to hiring someone she thinks may be gay. A different hiring manager in another office may have an excellent track record for fairly promoting women but borders on being named as a defendant in an age discrimination lawsuit.

In an ideal diversity working environment, to me, there is a uniform, fair, constantly evaluated and reasonably adjusted set of hiring criteria and hiring methods. While hiring standards that take place under one literal roof aren't necessarily better, being located in one building significantly increases the number of perspectives that are constantly evaluating the development and execution of fair employment practices.

## Numbers to Crunch

To achieve a perfect diversity workforce, you have to know what type of workers you employ. The numbers required by Equal Employment Opportunity (EEO) law are a good starting point for gauging this. What is EEO law? The EEO-1 Report is a survey that the U.S. government requires certain employers to complete, providing a numerical count of employees by job category and then by ethnicity, race, and gender. The report is submitted to the EEOC and the Department of Labor's Office of Federal Contract Compliance Programs (OFCCP). Employers with a federal government contract of $50,000 or more and fifty or more employees, and employers that do not have a federal government contract but have 100 or more employees, are required to complete an EEO-1 Report. (There are some exceptions.)

Keeping track of your employees using the criteria in the EEO-1 Report is a good place to begin, but this is just a starting point. In addition to keeping tabs on categories that people have no or almost no control over (such as race and gender), in my perfect diversity workplace, I would keep track of less obvious categories of difference. For example, I would have a rough idea of how many married, single, and divorced employees I had. I would want to know how many were parents whose kids were still at home, how many had no kids, and how many were parents whose kids were out of the nest. All this would give me an idea of whether my workplace had a balance of diversity regarding the marital and familial status of its employees.

Why would I want to know this? Because diversity in the workplace addresses the differences that people bring to work that either enhance their contributions or that can detract from their contributions, as a result of how their brand of difference weaves into the workplace. Any employer who has ever had employees with children complain about how their job is negatively affecting their work-life balance, while simultaneously dealing with employees without kids who are complaining that they are unfairly expected to pick up the slack of employees who have children, understands exactly the importance of those dynamics.

I could come up with dozens of different aspects of difference that help create a workplace seeping with parity—age, regional differences, education, military background, etc. In a perfect diversity workplace, difference and variety would not be rigid and artificial but would be greatly encouraged.

## Just the Starting Point

So we've got a perfect workplace. We've got a great, ergonomically constructed building. We've got flextime, fabulous, progressive benefits, and the kind of work environment that is written up in magazines. Applicants are lining up to be hired. But the numbers we've gathered are just a starting point.

One of the reasons why numbers aren't the only issue in building the perfect diversity workplace is that demographics can be measured only so far. People are more than the sum of their demographics, but even to the extent that the population characteristics can define your experience, demographics—at least some of them—can change. For example, at the time of this writing, I'm a black, heterosexual woman, over the age of forty, born and raised in the Midwest, with a bachelor's degree in journalism and a law degree, who has held careers as a newspaper reporter and as an employment attorney.

If someone picks up this book in two days or twenty years, if I am still alive, the demographics I've listed will not have changed. However, many other demographics, both positive and negative, could change: my marital status, my familial status, my physical abilities and disabilities, my economic class, my profession, the part of the country I live in, my spiritual/religious leanings, even elements of what seem like my basic personality.

We all have those demographic memberships that change, shift, and redefine themselves as we age. A perfect diversity workplace would easily accommodate the fluid nature of its workforce.

Another reason that numbers aren't the whole story is that numbers tell you nothing about the treatment that various groups receive. A workforce, for example, could have a sizable population of Chinese-American employees. But the numbers become less relevant if several complaints have been raised by those employees alleging discrimination or the number of employees isn't reflected in management as well as the rank and file.

## No Revolving Door of Complaints

In an ideal diversity workplace, employees don't bring ongoing, constantly revolving complaints of discrimination. This doesn't mean that the workplace will be complaint free. People will always have personality or work style conflicts that someone may think is based on unlawful discrimination.

But in this mythic, ideal workplace, when those rare allegations are made, personnel in human resources and the appropriate managers promptly and efficiently investigate the complaints without any preconceived notion about outcome. These managers deal appropriately with all parties involved in a way that communicates seriousness, dedication to the highest good of the entire workforce, and respect for both the accuser and the accused. When the process is finished, the outcome is held in confidence, but the tone continues to be set that this is a workplace where all employees have the job of upholding the standards that have been established if they want to continue to be employed in the workplace.

Doesn't it make you feel all warm and fuzzy to think about a workplace like that?

## Keys to Breaking This Chapter's Code

- There is no ideal workplace when it comes to diversity because the nature of diversity is always shifting in the workplace.

- If there was an ideal workplace when it comes to diversity, it would not put a cap on difference and it would allow for the fluid nature of demographics.

- Diversity isn't the only thing that changes in the workplace. An individual's blend of diversity can also change over time.

## Diversity Exercise

You are going to create your own diversity report card for the area of your job in which you are employed. For example, use your department or your job category, such as salesperson.

Write down five things you would rate your area on regarding diversity if you were judging. Don't give the area an actual rating—just create the categories. For example, one person's five areas might be: communication between different employees, diversity of people in management on the basis of race and gender, holidays that are selected to be paid holidays, mention of diversity in department newsletters, and number of complaints regarding diversity.

Then ask yourself: Why did you pick those categories and are any of them areas that can be judged just by looking at the numbers?

# CHAPTER FOURTEEN

# Is There Some Point Where My Company's Problem with Diversity Starts Being My Problem?

*Dear Diversity Diva:*

*I understand what you're saying about diversity and all. I get it. But I'm just middle management. I'm not having any problems. It's just the bosses who should care because they're the ones pulling down the big loot, right?*

*Signed,*
*I Rent, So the Trash in the Front Yard Ain't My Problem*

## Human Resources in Charge of Humans

When average people think of the HR department in the company where they work, they tend to think of the "resources" aspect of the function rather than the "human" part of it. People think of employee orientation, benefits, paychecks, training, evaluations, and all the multitude of rules and regulations that the department is responsible for.

But a big aspect of the department is dealing with the human element. It's managing the interactions and relationships that impact and form the workplace. It does not just mean being responsive to the problems that come up with employees but being proactive about issues that come up regarding diversity.

To a certain extent, some HR people have an obligation to observe the employment environment so that they can keep a vigilant gaze on whether any underlying issues exist that need to be addressed. When they do this as a routine part of their jobs, they gather information and become aware of the undercurrent of issues that exists. It is much more difficult for HR to do this when employees see HR people interacting with the rest of the company only when there is a problem or an investigation.

How can HR people observe without looking like they are being intrusive or outright spying? At company events, HR people could actually mingle more, introducing themselves and stepping out of the bubble. If a company doesn't have a lot of events—such as luncheons, discussion groups, after-work parties, or educational events—then HR could be more proactive in sponsoring them. Basically, HR should create opportunities for people to mingle, which would help HR to get the pulse of the work environment.

Also, if there are places where the employees in a company gather, HR people could make a point of actually going there too. For example, HR people could eat lunch in the company cafeteria, which would give them the opportunity to mix with others.

Again, the point isn't for HR to be nosy or attempt to conduct an investigation before a complaint has been filed. The point is for HR to be constantly in the habit of observing. Maybe every person in the department isn't a personality type well suited to do this, but in every company's HR department, someone needs to be. Then, HR would be aware of what's going on in the company. In every lawsuit regarding discrimination or harassment, there is almost always buzz going on before it snowballs into an actual complaint, let alone a lawsuit. In fact, in the Statement of Facts that is filed in the motion to the court to dismiss a case before it goes to trial, there is usually a fact or set of facts that makes you realize that there was a turning point in the circumstances leading up to the complaint. If some aware, objective person—removed from the situation or with a bit of authority—could have stepped in, she could possibly have derailed what eventually took place.

## Managers and Department Leaders Have to Actually Lead

Similar to the points made in the preceding section about the role of HR people, a lot of proactive responsibility falls on the heads of the men and women who are the frontline managers in the workplace. By frontline, I mean people who actually see the work of employees on a day-to-day or frequent basis. I mean the managers who see employees come to work at the beginning of their shifts, who see employees throughout the time they work, and who then see them when they leave.

How does a boss do that? By watching what goes on. For one thing, it's always a good idea not just to notice who bonds together but if there is a shift in bonding. I'm not talking about minute shifts, like Sally no longer going to lunch with Marquita. I'm talking about when, say, groups of a particular ethnic group, who normally seem to be smiling and laughing and talking freely, start looking pensive and serious and more concerned than usual about who may be listening to their conversations.

When you notice shifts like that, especially when they take place over more than just a day or two, then there may be something that requires a little probing. Maybe you can do this casually. When you have the opportunity, you could ask one of the group members whom you have a fairly open relationship with if there is something going on. It's not about stirring the pot or seeking gossip. It's about staying in touch with what is going on with your employees, especially if the issue even potentially has a problem attached.

People are very good at going up to a group of people who share some racial dynamic and trying to join in the conversation or comment on the gathering when the group is laughing or having fun. While there is nothing wrong with that if you're the type of manager who talks to these employees individually, this action is more likely to come off as intrusive and a nosy attempt to insert yourself into a rare opportunity for workers to relax and let down their guard for a few moments in the workplace.

Ultimately, the point is about managers and supervisors actually interacting with the people they manage in a way that invites trust and confidence. Most managers tend to fall into either of two extremes. They are way too distant from the people they manage, or they are so overly friendly that they destroy the healthy degree of boundaries that needs to be in place. Being a manager who is interested and approachable strikes the right balance for employees to come forward with their individual diversity issues that can have a larger impact on the work environment.

Managers who fail to observe, interact with, and act upon what they observe when necessary put themselves in the position of being the fall guy or girl when potential problems snowball. They will be questioned on what they knew and when they knew it. If you are a manager in charge of a department or area of your company that appears to have a problem, you will be questioned about what steps you took to prevent or lessen the issue. Also, because you are the manager, you will be held to a higher standard regarding what you did or didn't do than any other employee involved in the issue.

For example, say there is a female office worker who complains to the HR department that several male coworkers frequently make off-color, offensive comments and tell dirty jokes that make her feel uncomfortable. She tells HR that she has repeatedly told her coworkers to stop. While she hasn't reported this directly to her supervisor because she didn't feel comfortable doing so, HR should ask her manager what he observed. HR should ask if the manager ever observed the female worker's discomfort, overheard any jokes or comments, and was ever aware of any other female who expressed concern about the same issue.

In addition, a thorough HR investigator should probe a little deeper and try to get an idea of why the female coworker went directly to the HR department to register her complaint rather than going to her manager. It's not so much that HR is trying to blame the manager, but a sharp HR investigator goes the extra mile to make sure this isn't the surface of a larger problem. The investigator wants to make sure that the female employee's complaint is just an isolated issue. If HR doesn't look into these matters and the complaint keeps going, it will land right in the arms of the company's outside legal counsel, with massive billing rates. The attorneys will definitely ask these probing questions if the HR department doesn't.

So you see, managers and supervisors have a greater incentive than most in a company—even HR—to make sure they have their finger on the pulse of the diversity issues in the area that they govern. At the very least, they have a responsibility to create an environment with an open door, inviting employees to bring to them what they might not otherwise notice.

## High-Level Officers

Plaintiff attorneys love to depose high-level officers in discrimination lawsuits. There are more than a few reasons why this is so. One is that the further removed people are from the action, the more likely they are to spout off policies and platitudes about the company's commitment to diversity that a plaintiff attorney can then gleefully deconstruct one fact at a time based on the lawsuit being filed.

That's why the best witnesses in depositions for a company are the people who actually appear to have a handle on diversity in the organization. They are the vice presidents and CEOs and other top dogs who can cite actual diversity initiatives that they are personally involved in. These are the men and women who can give some indication that they truly have a top-down commitment to making sure that there are people with differences in the workplace, all having the same fair experiences, and that when a problem or issue has reared its ugly head, it's dealt with swiftly and fiercely.

Some companies hide behind glossy diversity brochures to obscure the fact that diversity is really a shell game in their company. Those companies may get awards and flattering magazine profiles, but employees are left going, as the old fast-food restaurant commercials from the 1980s used to say, "Where's the beef?"

So if high-ranking officials want their commitment to diversity to mean something, they have to actually pay as much attention to it as they do the financial aspects of their organization, the quality of their goods and services, and their marketing plan. Diversity has to be a visibly expressed value.

Like all employee relations issues, true diversity is something that should matter to top-level employees because it's the height of their integrity. Most people, deep down, believe that a company that treats either all its employees or segments of its employees like dirt won't hold the public that keeps them in business or that pays for the organization through taxes in any higher regard. Every company needs to recognize that diversity is just one aspect of being perceived as a trustworthy organization.

## Company Image Doesn't Always Tell the Real Deal

Everyone has worked for a company that has serious morale problems or worked at a terrific company where a small segment of employees had serious morale problems because an inept or oppressive supervisor was allowed to reign in unchecked terror. In either case, employees are always amazed at the press releases the company puts out about itself or the media coverage the company manages to attract.

I was at a diversity event where there was a table full of brochures from companies representing the industry hosting the event. A young minority student I had been talking to earlier came up to me as I was holding a brochure from a company that I had done some work for. She asked me about the people of color featured on the front of the brochure. I had to break the news to her that these weren't actual employees but actors/models who had been Photoshopped into the brochure. Another person standing by who worked for the company verified what I said.

The young woman looked so crushed that I almost felt bad for telling her. That's an example of how diversity is a constant advertising job. She wanted to see pictures of real employees who looked like her happily doing their jobs, and the fact that the photo was a fake made her question if that company's commitment to diversity was equally fake. The company's agenda may have been genuine, but the impression made by the false advertising may have caused the organization to lose a great job candidate.

## Diversity Doesn't Gloss Over Discrimination

There's diversity, and then there is discrimination and harassment. And if you have discrimination and harassment in your workplace, then it's everyone's problem.

Rank and file has to observe from the bottom up, just as management and supervisors have to observe from the top down. Everyone has to do this, because if even one person believes she is being treated unfairly because of her membership in a group, it affects the comfort level and trust of everyone in the workplace.

You may think, for example, that if a lesbian coworker is being discriminated against, it has nothing to do with you, since you are happily married and straight and don't even know anyone who is openly gay except for the people you see at work—but it does have something to do with you. It does if that woman does anything that affects your job. It affects you if that woman has several other coworkers in her corner who also think she is being discriminated against. It changes conversations, confidences, and trust; how people communicate and interact; what they share; and whom they share it with. People are tense. People are suspicious. Some people are angry. So yes, it affects you. It either affects you in small trickle-down fashion or impacts you like a torrential rush of rain generated by a tsunami.

That's why discrimination can be like a flu bug making its way around your office. It may not touch you yet, but if you hear enough people coughing, sooner or later, it will impact you.

## Keys to Breaking This Chapter's Code

- The human resources department needs to be more proactive in getting a read on the company's environment.

- Frontline managers have to pay more attention to what takes place with their workers since responsibility falls on their heads.

- Top managers need to make sure that diversity is more than just window dressing in their organization if they want to maintain credibility to the public.

## Diversity Exercise

If you've read this far into the book, you now know that one of the biggest keys to embracing diversity in your workplace is to become aware of what is going on around you. Nothing really ever seems like a person's concern until it personally affects him or until he is forcibly drawn into someone else's controversy.

Ask yourself if there is something—anything—even marginally related to diversity or some issue or problem with discrimination involving someone else that you could find yourself being questioned about as a witness. Strain the brain. Think about any comment, even one heard in passing or an observation made at the watercooler. Yes, gossip counts.

If there is even one thing, that's your tie to diversity in your workplace.

## Group Exercise

Have people break up in small groups to discuss their earliest memory of when they realized they were different or stood out in some way. Have individuals write down to discuss with the larger group the words that come to mind when they remember it. When people are in groups where they feel comfortable enough to be honest, it can be very powerful to see others talk with a lot of emotion about these types of events, which can range from being the first person of color in their school, to having kids tease them for stuttering, to being the poor kid involved in an activity when all the other kids come from money. Let this prompt a larger discussion about the pain or discomfort of being different in the workplace—in ways that are both obvious and not so obvious—and how it can have the same impact on adults as on kids. Then discuss the way those experiences and feelings can impact an entire department or work area.

# CHAPTER FIFTEEN

# When I See a Problem with Diversity, How Do I Go About Addressing It?

*Dear Diversity Diva:*

*I see things going on around me left and right that I know HR or somebody around here should be dealing with. I know that as a manager, it's part of my job to deal with it. I don't want to rock the boat since this rickety little ship puts food on my family's table. But I just can't sit here anymore. What do I do?*

*Signed,*
*Sitting Still in Choppy Waters*

## The Man (or Woman) in the Mirror

When it comes to diversity in any setting, but particularly the workplace, the things we notice are the things that we probably most need to work on ourselves. (This is not always so. Sometimes the flip is also true—the things that we are completely oblivious to, until someone points them out, are also the things that we may most need to pay attention to.)

For example, you are friendly with a coworker, Sara, who always makes snide comments about another coworker, Emmanuel, who speaks with a foreign accent. On the one hand, Sara's comments are mean and rude. But on the other hand, you laugh at them because you find them funny. You're in a trick bag of sorts—you know what Sara says is wrong, but you're friendly with her and don't have any kind of friendly relationship with Emmanuel.

In this situation, there is only one thing you can do. You must choose to not go along with behavior that you know is wrong. You can do this in two ways. If you are an assertive type of person, you can say, "Look, it's not funny to make fun of how Emmanuel speaks, so let's not do that anymore, okay?" However, many people seem to operate from the philosophy that any kind of direct commentary, no matter how nicely said, is confrontation, and confrontation is to be avoided at all cost.

So, if you're not the kind of person who would go for the direct approach, you can choose not to laugh or join in the next time Sara makes a joke about Emmanuel's accent. Most of the time, nothing stops an off-color joke more quickly than silence on the part of the person hearing it. Sure, there is the occasional clueless, rude, or bigoted person who tries to make you the bad guy for failing to join in on offensive comments. But fewer improper jokes and comments would be passed along if at some point in the chain, someone just didn't perpetuate the offense by hitting the "forward" button or pulling someone aside to pass it on.

In some workplaces, for example, it is against company policy for an employee to even respond to an offensive e-mail. While I think that policy can be a little harsh in situations where someone is merely writing back, "Please don't send this mess to me at work anymore!" I think the spirit of the policy is spot on—that responding to offensive behavior oftentimes encourages it, even unintentionally.

When you notice a problem at work, it triggers something you need to do in response. As had been previously stated, people don't work in isolation. They work with other people, and what affects one often affects all.

## Isolated Issues: Ignore, Store, or Implore

Isolated issues in the workplace can be a bit trickier to deal with. People don't want to feel as if they are running around being the Thought Police, where every single comment or word needs to be dealt with, no matter how much long-term discomfort or awkwardness is caused.

As with all things involving good judgment in the workplace, it's a matter of weighing the severity of the offense with other important elements that balance out the situation. For example, you may choose to pretend not to have heard anything if someone pretty low on the workplace food chain, whom you've never heard utter an offensive word before, says something that you know would offend others and get him in trouble if others heard. Sure, there is the philosophy that you're part of the problem if you're not part of the solution. But that's not always how it works in the place where you collect your check.

It's one thing when you're dealing with an educated person in an organization who has a big title and enough authority to know exactly what she shouldn't be saying or doing. But it's different if you're dealing with someone you know is limited in education or experience and whom you do not have that close a relationship with. In that case, saying something to her about one misstep of the mouth won't necessarily get your point across and may do more harm than good. Ignoring this one-time issue may be the thing to do.

For some, the concept of ignoring an issue like this could be controversial, especially since managers are usually trained regarding the importance of documenting infractions. Ultimately, as a leader, you have to weigh the conditions and rules of your particular workplace to decide the degree to which you may ignore an isolated issue.

However, along with ignoring the isolated comment or incident comes the part where you store it away. This is important because an isolated incident will no longer be isolated if the person continues on the path of that behavior. That's where storing the information becomes necessary. If in the future you need to confront the person or report her behavior, you can provide additional context, support, and examples for what you are bringing up.

If you think an isolated issue comes from a person you believe has the capacity to hear what you are saying, then you should have a crucial conversation with him. The concept of crucial conversations has become popular in the workplace organizational field because it is the skill of having a difficult conversation with someone in a way that is effective and productive without being offensive. After all, you don't want to cause more offense in dealing with someone else's behavior that you find offensive.

Sometimes you can't help offending the person, because the very nature of raising something that she will take as criticism will offend her. But as long as you are doing your part to operate from a sense of integrity, then your focus shouldn't be derailed by her response.

Therefore, when someone in your workplace makes an isolated offensive comment or derogatory remark about a group of people or a specific person based on his membership in a specific group, you have to decide whether you are going to ignore it, store it until time gives you more information to evaluate, or implore the person to recognize that in this incident she has said something that offends.

## Ongoing Issues Require Immediate Action

An ongoing issue by its very nature means that it is not isolated. Therefore, ignoring it isn't an option.

With cases like this, you probably have been storing observations for a while. Perhaps you are personally on the receiving end of negative actions, or you are observing what is happening to others. Maybe you think you're being discriminated against because of your gender, age, race, national origin, sexual orientation, religion, or some other reason. Maybe it's not even something that you're sure has a legal basis, but you feel there is something going on in your workplace that has a negative impact. You know that it is not fair and that it is impacting the workplace, and you suspect that it's not based on anything legitimate or work-related.

Regardless, your only option—depending on the severity of what you are observing and the impact it is having on your job—is taking it to someone who can actually do something about the issue. In some cases, that is your direct supervisor. (It probably goes without saying that if you yourself are a manager or have any type of direct or indirect human resources role in your company, your response is going to be to deal with any diversity infractions you personally observe an employee engage in. You just don't have the option to ignore it.)

Depending on exactly what the problem is, you may not need to be very formal in your informing. It might be a passing "Hey, have you noticed how tensed up the women get whenever Jim tells one of his little jokes?" or "I know you want me to work on this project with Delia, but she has a way of interjecting comments about my age that kind of bothers me."

When issues are more pressing—comments or references that leave no room for misunderstanding on the seriousness of their offense—then a more formal statement or complaint needs to be made.

Once upon a time in the world of employment law, the only person whom you could make a report to about discriminatory matters was your supervisor, so if your supervisor was the source of the problems or the alleged discrimination, you were—to use the highly regarded legal term—screwed. As often happens over the years, decades, and sometimes centuries, the law caught up to how the world really operates. Now, people have the option of going to someone other than their immediate boss to make a formal complaint. Often, that alternative option is the human resources department.

Now, granted, that is so much easier said than done. When you are on the receiving end of discrimination or you're observing something going down with someone else, you get self-conscious, bordering on paranoid. You're afraid to e-mail anyone about this, because it leaves a trail. You worry about calling someone on the phone, even if you have your own office, because you're afraid someone else will overhear. And for sure, you have zero desire to be seen actually walking into the HR department.

But if it gets to the point where that is what you need to do, the more paranoid you are, the more important it is for you to do just that. You do what you have to do—just exercise good judgment and vigilance. Maybe you e-mail an HR person using your personal e-mail address from home. Or you find an empty office and use the phone there.

If the concerns involve you personally, you have no choice but to handle it that way because the law is clear. You have to give your employer an opportunity to investigate and resolve an issue before you file a lawsuit, if it ever gets serious enough to require that.

## Affinity Groups as Workplace Resources

Most challenges, issues, or problems regarding diversity don't rise to the level of you needing to either deal with an individual employee or file a complaint. Many times, the issues are far subtler. Therefore, if it's a general problem with diversity—like the company not hiring enough members of a group or the company being a revolving door for a particular group so none seek to stay—then seek out a workplace diversity committee member or see about joining an affinity group.

An affinity group is an employer-endorsed employee resource group created around shared membership, with the most common ones being race, gender, and sexual orientation. (Some people find these groups controversial because they can reek of self-imposed segregation.) A big reason for the existence of affinity groups is that even when there isn't a problem, people with particular issues like to bond to improve their situation or discuss matters that are unique to them.

For example, if a group of mothers in the workplace has an affinity group, its purpose isn't to exclude men or women who aren't mothers. Rather, it's to provide a sounding board and a resource to enhance the mothers' work experience.

Those who aren't "in the club," so to speak, may resent that a company supports certain segments of workplace difference but not others. Ideally, I think a company should support any affinity group whose purpose is to enhance the experience of employees and make them better contributors to the organization. For example, supporting an affinity group for employees who golf may not be a good use of company resources. But an affinity group for working dads might be a good idea and just what the organization needs, because the issues of men who have to juggle their parenting duties with their work duties may well be relevant to the company. Men can gather support and ideas from each other in a way that makes them more productive, less stressed-out employees when they are at work.

The other controversial point about affinity groups is that while technically, all employees should be able to attend and join a group, regardless of whether they are part of that group's focus, people need to understand that the conversation changes if "outsiders" are there. The majority of people in the group, who have limited time to express their concerns, have to spend a lot of time defending or even just explaining their issues to someone on the outside. For example, let's say I attend an affinity group for employees who are disabled when I am not myself disabled, just because I want to be supportive. I might well bog down a meeting by expressing comments or asking questions regarding issues that everyone in the room already understands. Even if I don't say a word, I may be carrying an air or be perceived as carrying an air of paternalistic superiority because the other people in the room can't figure out why I'm even there.

When doing the book tour for my first book, *Working While Black,* I often encountered a white, male, middle-aged colleague who wanted to attend certain events that were sponsored by black organizations or book-stores. He would repeatedly get offended when I said that he couldn't come, because people coming to those events with questions or concerns would find the conversation instantly changed with him in the room. On occasion, he would show up anyway, and I could tell that there were people who felt stifled, suspicious, and even occasionally angry by his presence. To them, it felt that the one time they had an opportunity to openly express issues, they still had to worry about who was in the room.

My colleague's motivation was admirable. He truly wanted to learn and understand. However, when people have limited time and opportunity to address their own diversity issues, they do not want to feel as if someone is learning on "their" time.

Companies should do more to bring affinity groups together, along with the rest of the workforce occasionally, to demystify the groups' existence and encourage support for them.

## Keys to Breaking This Chapter's Code

- Noticing that there is always a choice in how you handle a tricky diversity issue is the first step in handling it properly.

- When someone offends in the workplace on an isolated basis, the options are to ignore it, store it to see if it happens again, or implore the person not to repeat the offensive act. Ongoing issues, however, need to be dealt with immediately.

- Affinity groups are a resource that helps various groups deal proactively with the particular issues involving their workplace experiences.

## Diversity Exercise

Assuming that you personally don't have a discrimination complaint to file (if you do, you need to follow the reporting policy of your company to the letter to make sure all your rights and legal defenses are preserved), think about what practical and accessible resources are available to you if you want to express concerns about diversity issues at your job.

Read your company newsletter closely to see if there is a diversity committee or officer or various affinity groups. Visit your company's website to see if there is some point guard for diversity that you don't know about. Casually ask fellow employees how they handle these types of issues.

Be creative when you write the resources down on paper. But use good judgment if you feel inspired to address a workplace issue using one of the resources on your list.

# CHAPTER SIXTEEN

# Isn't Instituting Real Change Bound to Tick Someone Off?

*Dear Diversity Diva:*

*It just seems safer to leave everything the way it is. Maybe things aren't perfect, but people should just be grateful to have their jobs when times are tough. Surely you agree that there are times when it's best to just let everything be, no matter had bad it gets for a few?*

*Signed,*
*Head in the Sand Can Be Comfortable*

## Change Is Risk

Change can be risky to people. That's not groundbreaking analysis, but it's one of those things that is much easier said than accepted. And changing the status quo when it comes to diversity in the workplace is the one time you know you tick someone off.

Statistics say that by the year 2042, the composition of the United States will tilt toward white Americans not being in the numerical majority. I say "numerical" deliberately because numbers don't tell the whole story of what this will mean in terms of the balance of power and how that will play out in the workplace. Also, these numbers don't tell us what this change means about any demographic other than race. It doesn't tell us the impact it will have on those other numbers.

So yes, many things will change between now and when that day comes. When many people—even nonwhites—hear that statistic, they wonder what that change will mean, and in wondering about the great unknown, they fear it.

That's just the way change hits the average person, a twist on the old adage that the "devil you *know* is better than the devil you don't know."

However, long before we get to that degree of overarching societal change, we can see how people react to even piecemeal change along the way. If you've worked long enough, you can remember the reactions that people had when they got their "first" in a new supervisor—the first woman in a role always performed by men, the first man in a role always performed by women, the first member of a certain ethnic group, the first openly gay person, the first person with a disability, etc. Even if it wasn't a significant demographic first, think about how people acted when someone was hired with a college degree when the previous people in that job never had one, or vice versa. Or think about the first time a top official in the company was hired from outside the company or hired from out-of-town.

While change isn't always risky and some people downright thrive on it, any disruption in the World According to How You Have Always Known It to Be can trigger a bit of anxiety as you wonder how that change will impact you.

That's why being a voice in the workplace wilderness who decides to shine a spotlight on a tricky issue regarding diversity can make you a source of change, which you may not want to bring upon yourself. Most who take the risk of raising a problem of discrimination or unfair treatment know that the spotlight is going to shine brighter on them than on the actual issue or problem being brought up.

Because of that aversion to change or being the agent of change, many people handle it by just leaving. They leave the department, the company, or sometimes even the industry. Or they stay, grit their teeth, swallow their emotions in front of the bosses, vent to trusted confidants every chance they get, and let themselves be eaten up inside until layoff, death, retirement, or divine intervention ends the cycle for them.

## Next to Change, the Biggest Workplace Sin Is Discomfort

The nature of diversity is that the people with the status of majority dominance don't like to feel uncomfortable or deal with any change that upsets that balance.

Dominance can sound like a dirty word—a word loaded with the imagery of oppression, unchecked power, twisted greed, and arrogance. But that's not how I mean it in this context at all. I mean dominance in terms of membership in the group that has the distinct edge in terms of numbers, acceptance, and instant credibility when it comes to "rights."

Dominance comes in all kinds of forms even though the first thing that pops into the minds of most people is "white" or "male." However, there are a multitude of ways that dominance shows up in the workplace. Dominance, for example, can show up where almost every person in a department is married with school-age children, so whenever there is a project or event that requires long hours or an expectation of weekend work, it gets shoved toward the single, childless employee with the reasoning that "she doesn't have a family so it's no big deal."

Another example is the flip of the previous example, where a married worker with school-age children is in a department full of young, single party animals who don't mind working late because it just makes it easier to go to happy hour together. In this particular example of dominance, the employee who needs to get off work on time to get home and start dinner clearly understands who has the dominant value system in that workplace.

Another word for dominance that has the same uncomfortable ring but gets to the same point is *privilege*. For example, many in the gay and lesbian community talk about how people generally can take for granted heterosexual privilege, where the world caters to the assumption of "straight" in terms of language, policy, laws, rules, etc. However, if you make that point to a large enough group of people, someone will make a statement to the effect of "But straight people are the majority so what's the big deal since one can't always include everyone?" Oftentimes, I find that the people who make that kind of statement are (1) beneficiaries of the privileged group being talked about and (2) usually pretty quick to notice how their interests are marginalized in some other group they are a member of.

Which gets to the heart of one of the truths about diversity: recognizing and admitting to the ways that each and every person—in some way—is privileged in this society and how society and the workplace cater to that privilege.

If you look around your particular workplace and really pay attention, you can see a whole host of privileged groups, where a disruption of that balance could easily be rocked. In the nursing field, for example, most workplaces are dominated by women, so determining how to address issues that come up usually starts from the assumption that women and the needs of female employees are what need to be addressed.

But what happens in a hospital where one of the few male nurses wants to take a leave of absence—either under the Family and Medical Leave Act or a paid leave under company policy—because his wife had a baby and he wants to take three months off to stay home with the baby when his wife goes back to work? When he meets resistance or outright hostility, is it because he has asked for something different from his coworkers who had a new baby, or is it because he is not in the privileged group whose needs dominate?

The thing about privilege or dominance (or whatever word you come up with to help you understand the point) is that it takes a deliberate consciousness to look at the ways in which you as an individual or as a member of a group are in the group of dominance. If you take that brave leap, then you have to consider that maybe everything that has come your way wasn't based on merit or "just the way things are." Also, you may have to give legitimacy to or acknowledge the issues of the folks who aren't in your group.

Some years ago, a white woman named Peggy McIntosh—who is a professor at Wellesley College in Massachusetts—wrote a paper titled "White Privilege, Color and Crime: A Personal Account."[1] She defined privilege as "an invisible package of unearned assets which I can count on cashing in every day, but about which I was 'meant' to remain oblivious."

McIntosh hits the nail on the head about how privilege, as a basis of power, isn't something that one is supposed to be consciously aware of or to consciously utilize. That makes it different from the power we associate with "the privileged class" of people, who consciously use their wealth and status to shape their lives in a deliberate way, regardless of how it affects others.

Another critical point to make is that almost everyone is a member of a group that benefits from unconscious privilege even when he or she is also a member of a group that is simultaneously disadvantaged in the same workspace. For example, a white woman who is feeling the double standard attached to being a woman, which negatively impacts her work experience compared to the men in her workplace, may not see the ways that being white gives her advantages compared to the minority women doing the same job.

Another example is where members of a racial minority can clearly see how whites in their department are treated with greater leniency when problems come up. But they don't see how much accommodation is made for them when family issues come up, compared to the people at their job who don't have families.

## How Does Leadership Communicate Change?

One of the primary jobs for managers and HR leaders is to be available to listen to and deal with the gripes of employees. It might not be listed quite that directly in the job description, but that's exactly what the job requires.

So, since that is the case, one of the first steps to take if you are a leader or manager of any kind is to check in with yourself to see how you truly feel about diversity improvement. Are you generally fine with the concept of diversity? Are there specific aspects of it that you have a problem with? Are there certain groups of people that you have a problem with? Is the way your company handles diversity issues something you feel any kind of discomfort over? Worse, are you experiencing resentment?

It is important to ask these questions of yourself (and to give honest answers right back) because in addition to being the filter and investigator of change in the workplace, you have to be the communicator of change. Sometimes the people at the top of the organization don't communicate the importance of diversity in a way that convinces employees that they truly find it important. Or more often, top managers communicate it because they truly do believe in diversity as a company value—but the frontline managers who are in charge of enforcing diversity initiatives in day-to-day ways show resistance or outright defiance.

Or (as I've addressed throughout this book) the managers may believe in diversity when it comes to certain kinds of groups but not to others. For example, female leaders may be particularly supportive of diversity initiatives that address the concerns and issues of women, but those same leaders may block diversity improvement when it comes to certain ethnic groups. Or there may be leaders who are members of certain ethnic groups but have no ability to understand that supporting diversity on the issue of race also requires the same commitment to fair treatment when dealing with employees who, for example, have emigrated here from other countries.

One way to check yourself on that issue is to take a periodic survey, either formally or informally. Ask your employees what they hear when the company communicates its diversity objectives or initiatives or results. Ask your employees if they feel that diversity initiatives apply to some members of your workforce but not to others. Find out if your employees believe that there is integrity behind your words. And more critical than asking all these hard questions, really *listen* to what they say. Listen for the topics, the issues, the false assumptions, and the true assumptions that require follow-up. And listen to what they *don't* say.

## Real Issues vs. Illusion

Oftentimes, seemingly with the tiniest diversity issue, workplace leaders are required to do more than look at what seems to be the issue. They need to poke beneath the glossy, distracting surface to see what real issue is taking place. For example, say you are a manager and an employee complains that she has an issue with a cartoon in the company newsletter. She makes some joke to you about how she finds it offensive. Rather than blowing the complaint off as that of an oversensitive employee or as someone just making a passing comment, you need to probe a little deeper. Ask her exactly what she's offended by because sometimes a passing comment is just that, and sometimes it's part of a much more complicated context.

Follow up on what she is saying to see if she's pointing to some wider issue in the workplace. Is she saying, perhaps, that this is not an isolated issue of offense or that it points to a general insensitivity regarding a specific group? Is she bringing this up because she really is having an issue with a supervisor or a coworker?

And when seemingly small issues like this come up, it's important to document (not necessarily in the employee's file) that the issue was raised and addressed. Often when more significant issues come up down the line and an employee files a complaint over a large issue of discrimination, she points to all the "little" things that she brought to management's attention that management failed to deal with.

I don't want to promote the approach that all issues of diversity lead to claims of discrimination. But almost all claims of discrimination have misplaced handling of diversity issues as their genesis. That's why there is no such thing as a small matter in dealing with issues of diversity. That may appear to contradict what I said earlier, in Chapter 15, about ignoring isolated issues, but the truth of diversity is that evolving issues aren't always that clear-cut. That's why paying attention all the time and not just when things are being investigated is a key aspect of managing diversity.

## The Power of Empowerment

Some fear that empowering people to know their rights or express them through diversity initiatives makes people more likely to sue, file complaints, or just stir up the pot. Actually, a company that makes employees feel like they have a way to express and assert their rights within the boundaries of a legitimate workplace framework is probably more likely to deal with employee issues in ways that don't lead to unchecked complaint filing.

For one thing, you are giving people an avenue of expression that allows them to feel that they can come to management when there is a problem, as opposed to employers that leave individuals feeling as if they are always fending for themselves. Labor unions can be controversial to some, but the concept of collective bargaining has the right spirit in wanting to make sure that all employees have a voice that is heard by management—which is a large part of managing diversity properly, allowing all employees to feel that, when appropriate, they have been heard.

## Values of an Organization

When it gets down to it, companies have to ask themselves what they truly value and if workplace diversity is one of those values. If so, that value comes at a price—the risk that not every employee will sign off on it as a priority.

However, every company has the right—actually, the duty, if it wants to succeed in good times and bad—to have a core set of values that the company should be centered on. And these values need to be communicated from the time before a prospective employee even agrees to join the workforce.

Therefore, if as a company you are going to boldly state and mean that diversity is a core value of your workplace, there should never be a pass on any opportunities to enforce it. (There's a difference between an individual ignoring a truly isolated, fleeting, misspoken word that has no wide impact and a company ignoring a diversity issue, not matter how small it appears to be.) Just like every company effectively communicates that employees aren't allowed to steal, lie, or damage the reputation of the company, so too does the value of diversity need to be endorsed that clearly.

## Keys to Breaking This Chapter's Code

- Change is risky, and instituting a company-endorsed improvement in diversity matters will be perceived as change.

- In the workplace, there is almost always a way that every employee benefits from being a member of a dominant or privileged group.

- The values of an organization determine its priorities and successes, with diversity existing as a value that a company has to actively choose to make important.

## Diversity Exercise

Think of a news event that you had a very strong, emotional reaction to. Maybe it's a crime story involving a famous person. Maybe it's a political story. The key is that you have to have had extremely strong opinions about it (even if you don't want to characterize yourself as having had an emotional reaction).

Challenge yourself to think why you took the position you did. Test yourself to see if there were similar situations with similar facts that didn't trigger the same reaction. Ask yourself: Why?

Here's a controversial example: Let's say you had a particularly strong reaction to the O. J. Simpson trial. Keep asking yourself "why" questions about this, and then challenge the answers. If your answer is "Because two people were murdered," then ask yourself if there is any other case involving people being murdered that you had an equally strong opinion about. If your answer is "Because he is a celebrity and I admired him at one point," and then ask yourself if you had the same reaction when any other famous person was accused of a crime.

After you have taken yourself as far as you can go with that opinion, truly put yourself in the shoes of a person who had a completely different point of view. (Remember, it's just a mental exercise that no one has to know anything about but you—or me, if you decide to send me an e-mail and tell me about it.)

Ask yourself, for example, why a black person would want to believe that Simpson didn't commit the murder. Ask yourself why blacks in general seem to defend Simpson. Don't just stop with the easy answer. Keep putting yourself in that person's place and come up with a reason that's in the neighborhood of making sense to you.

## Note

1.  Peggy McIntosh, "White Privilege, Color and Crime: A Personal Account," Working Paper #189, Wellesley College Center for Research on Women, 1988.

# CHAPTER SEVENTEEN

# If I'm the One Being Accused of Cultural Insensitivity or Worse, Aren't I Already Screwed?

*Dear Diversity Diva:*

*I just got tapped in a complaint that one of my subordinates brought against me. I didn't do anything wrong but that's pretty irrelevant now. The accusation alone will ruin my career, won't it?*

*Signed,*
*Burnt Toast*

## What Exactly Am I Being Accused of Again?

Some think that because they are being accused of cultural insensitivity, it means that they are being accused of discrimination. It doesn't necessarily mean that, but if the accusation of cultural insensitivity isn't addressed or dealt with, then over time, the allegation of discrimination or bigotry could arise. When such an accusation is not addressed or acknowledged, the comment or question can fester in the mind of the person who is offended. It particularly festers if the person talks about it with someone who is in the same group as him. When that happens, the words or behavior can take on a life of their own.

For example, if you ask people from a different ethnic group what it is that they "do" with their hair, it can be one of those instances where you are asking the question because you really don't know. You may think that asking the question is just making a general inquiry along the lines of "Where did you buy that coat you're wearing because my son is looking for one like it?" However, there's a chance that the question may come off as culturally insensitive to the people on the receiving end. It may sound more like you're asking a zookeeper what kind of bamboo a panda bear eats than asking a fellow human being to share a beauty secret.

These kinds of missteps happen every day in the workplace. One person says something, just meaning to start conversation, or makes a backhanded comment or even a compliment, and it gets analyzed and re-analyzed for its "true" meaning.

Some people may say that the tendency of others to take things the wrong way comes from a society that has become overly sensitive. But what those same people fail to realize is that the individuals who wonder what someone "really" meant by a statement or question have been on the receiving end of that kind of cultural disconnect for years. As I've frequently said to people over the years, people aren't always right in their perception of whether something is discriminatory or offensive, but that doesn't mean that they are always incorrect either, especially when the perception comes from walking every day in different shoes than you do. If not in the workplace, then personally or through the media, there is not a group in America—including every majority group—that has not found offense in the way it is portrayed in the entertainment media or some other venue.

For example, any employee with a physical disability of some kind has most likely had a curious, sometimes well-meaning coworker whom he doesn't know all that well ask an intrusive and inappropriate question about how his disability affects his personal life.

At least once in their lives, no matter how high their status in an organization, almost all members of minority ethnic groups have had someone make a presumption, however innocently intended, about their group. Unfortunately, these comments often come from members of other minority groups. These people don't realize that being members of a minority group doesn't mean that their comments or questions won't cause offense to be taken. (Just recently, for example, my friend and I were eating out at a buffet. We were the only blacks in the restaurant. A stranger walked up to our table and told an offensive joke about blacks and Jews, ending it with, "I'm Jewish so I can tell that joke." He had the mistaken assumption that if a Jew tells a joke to a black person about blacks and Jews, that cancels out the offense. No, it doesn't, particularly if you're making that assumption about a complete stranger.)

## Defensiveness Is Not a Defense

People always have a right to point out when your words or behavior offends them. That simple little statement trips a lot of people up. They want to debate it, resist it, argue with it. Or worse, they agree with it up to the point that there are words or behavior that they believe shouldn't "logically" offend someone.

When it comes to making money, companies know that defensiveness is irrelevant. For example, in the 1970s, American Motors came out with a car called the Matador. A great deal of time, money, and research went into the car. In most places where the car was sold, the hope was that the name would evoke the virility of a bullfighter. Unfortunately, in Puerto Rico, the literal translation was *killer*, and Puerto Rico at the time had a problem with excessive driving fatalities. I'm sure executives and people from the marketing team apologized profusely. But the bottom line was that sales of the car in Puerto Rico were low.

Although there was no intent to offend, that was still a result from the company's action. Intent, even when innocent, does matter—and sometimes bad results are the end game of neutral, benign causes put into motion.

Therefore, when it comes to issues of diversity, to understanding where people are coming from, results and impact do matter. And it's only in understanding why someone takes offense that you get the understanding that might help you get a grasp on stopping a problem before it snowballs out of control, since it's not enough to merely state repeatedly that you didn't mean to offend.

Also, getting to the heart of understanding may help prevent you from making the same mistake in the future. Because the next time it happens, as with all similar offenses or offenses stemming from the same misunderstanding or assumptions, you can't say you didn't know. The next time it happens, people will assume willful intent.

Again, in certain situations, intent matters. The nature of the intent or the recklessness of the behavior may buy you a little less blame, but not much. It's the difference between deliberately mowing someone down with your car because you want to kill him and he dies, and getting behind the wheel after eight shots of tequila with no concern about what might happen and someone dies. In both cases, if someone ends up dead, you will be charged with murder. It's just a matter of whether it will be first degree murder or some version of manslaughter. In the case of manslaughter, not having the intent to kill someone doesn't mean you get to act like it doesn't count, just because you didn't get behind the wheel with the mental mind-set of causing someone's death.

While offenses of diversity don't, of course, rise to the level of manslaughter, the analogy is given here to show that even in the most serious of matters, intent may matter, but willful, knowing, deliberate, purposefully framed effort to cause harm does not always have to be in play. They say that ignorance of the law is no excuse. When it comes to diversity, ignorance may be an excuse, but it's not one that gets you very far.

## The Two Things to Say When You've Caused Offense

When someone causes offense in matters of diversity, there are two things to say.

### Saying You're Sorry

In some way, shape, or form, the first thing is "I'm sorry you took offense to what I said [or did]." In saying that, you are not necessarily admitting to being wrong. This is a distinction that many do not comprehend. The common perspective on saying the word "sorry" in any fashion is that you are saying, "I'm wrong." From a cultural communication standard, many men generally seem particularly conditioned to view any version of "I'm sorry" as complete capitulation.

But when you say that you are sorry that someone felt offended by what you said or did, all you really are saying is that you regret that your words or actions caused negative impact on another. And the biggest thing to be clear on is that you are saying you are sorry because of the impact.

It's similar to when you are in a grocery store and your cart accidentally hits another cart while you're looking in another direction for a moment. You reflexively say, "I'm sorry," not because you deliberately rammed your cart into the other person's cart but because your little slice of human space accidentally bumped someone else's human space as a result of your unintentional moment of inattentiveness. That simple, three-second act of acknowledging the accidental bump usually keeps a ten-second encounter at ten seconds.

## Asking Why Someone Was Offended

In workplace dynamics regarding matters of cultural disconnect or diversity, obviously, issues are often a little more complex than the shopping cart example, for a couple of reasons. One, because there is an ongoing work relationship taking place where another person may have a whole assortment of opinions about you that influence how he took the comment, and two, because words are often perceived to be more purposeful and therefore more hurtful in their impact.

So, in those matters where you "bump your coworker's cart," in addition to making an apology, you underscore your meaning—rather than admitting guilt to some purposeful harm—by the next thing that comes out of your mouth. When you have caused offense, a good next place to go is asking, "Can you explain to me why you are offended?" Sometimes, of course, the answer is obvious, such as if you used an epithet against someone's group membership. Other times, further inquiry is required.

The key thing in this situation is to not get caught up in the drama of reacting to the accusation that you have offended someone. Even though the accusation could escalate into a full-blown complaint and investigation at some point, that's even more of a reason why maintaining a cool head is important because the very words you use in the heat of an exchange could later come back to haunt you. The average sane person doesn't get angry or defensive when accidental physical contact takes place. I say this not to be dismissive of feelings but to point out that people are human. Things come out of people's mouths that can be insensitive, hurtful, and sometimes downright bigoted. And unfortunately, many times people are clueless about the effect of what they are saying. My point is that a cool head should prevail whether it's an accidental physical contact or an accidental offensive comment.

More often than people realize, employees at work have been known to get into actual fistfights because of misunderstandings. According to the Occupational Safety and Health Administration, there are approximately 2 million incidents a year of workplace violence in the United States, so the importance of encouraging people to keep reactions manageable is no small issue. It isn't just about minimizing their feelings. It's about maintaining a safe environment when things go astray.

## Personal Labels Are Not Allowed

When it comes to offense, it may seem that the person who said the words or engaged in the behavior has all the responsibility to resolve or clean up the situation, while the person who was offended has none because he is the "victim." But that's not the case at all in situations where the offense isn't clear-cut. If there is any room for interpretation, then the offended person bears a little bit of responsibility in explaining—not defending or needing to justify but in explaining—what exactly it is that he is offended by and why.

Again, apologizing and seeking to understand offense go a long way toward healing or at least neutralizing any harm created by the words or behavior at issue.

## Proving a Negative

It is extremely difficult—impossible really—to prove a negative, so people need to exercise great care when they label the person rather than labeling the behavior.

I know someone who is a professional, white-collar employee who works a retail job nights and weekends to help pay for two children in college. On an average shift of his extra job, he interacts with several hundred members of the public, with a significant percentage of the customers being lower income members of a different race than he is. He is hands-down one of the most humane, good-hearted people anyone could ever know. Yet at least once every few weeks, one of the customers, in a fit of irritation, accuses him of being a racist because a transaction goes poorly—usually something beyond his control like a debit card getting turned down or an item not ringing up properly.

He asked me once, "How do I prove that I'm not a racist? I'm not!" If he wasn't so sincerely earnest in his question, it might be amusing, but it's not amusing. It's not at all. Accusing someone of being a bigot (a much broader accusation than that of being a racist) is a horrible weapon to use against someone unless you mean it with all your heart and it's based on actual actions and words that the person has committed, usually over time.

My advice to my friend, as it is to anyone in that position, is that you can't prove a negative and shouldn't even try when the accusation has been lodged against you in a fit of isolated anger based on a limited, sporadic interaction with someone you have no ongoing relationship with.

If you drive and ever have to drive in a big city, there will be times when someone you accidentally cut off gives you the middle finger and calls you something that requires a bar of soap shoved in her mouth. You wouldn't follow that person home and give her a list of references to prove that you're really a considerate person. Just like that, you can't singlehandedly dismantle every accusation of bigotry that comes your way in the workplace if they're made in a pique of anger.

If you're the person who feels offended, the flip side of that is that you can't go leveling the bomb of "You're a racist" [or sexist or homophobe or whatever applicable bigoted label applies] every time you're angry. For one, it's an awful thing to say to someone in those instances where it's just not true. In addition, it reduces your credibility on that point for future instances when you may have to whole-heartedly make that claim.

It's just too important to not get in the bad habit of always jumping to the personal label whenever there is a problem. For example, I can always say "I'm offended," but calling someone a racist or a bigot is a whole different story. The difference is that no one else can define your feelings but you. But once you call someone a name, you are trying to singlehandedly label and define who another human being is. It isn't your right to do so even when you think you're 100 percent right.

## Two Wrongs Don't Make a Right, Just a Wide U-Turn

As upsetting as it may be to be accused of insensitivity, you can't let it justify your doing the wrong thing in retaliation out of defensiveness or anger.

I once met a business owner who was sued by an employee for religious discrimination. From that point forward, he hired only independent contractors in his company, including his vice president. While that may have technically been something that he was allowed to do in the state he operated out of, this approach did not build morale, inspire loyalty, or in any way contribute to the positive working environment that most successful businesses aim to create. In addition, he was not necessarily protecting himself legally, but that's another issue.

Another form of retaliation (and I'm not talking here about the legal cause of action for retaliation, which has very specific elements to be a cause of action) is to strike back at the person by saying "You're the bigot" whenever someone accuses you of committing an offense. If you're leveling that comment because you truly feel that way, based on an ongoing course of conduct, that's one thing. But firing back with that is just a childish game of "I Know I Am But What Are You" that serves no purpose in the workplace.

## Seeking Help When Necessary

It is important to not take it personally when someone calls you some variation of bigot in the workplace or to immediately attempt to convince him on the spot that you're not. But that doesn't mean that you should completely let it go.

In almost any situation where that accusation has been raised, the key thing is to extract yourself from the emotions of the moment, calm down if you're upset, and then report the problem to your supervisor, the supervisor of your fellow employee, or the HR department. As uncomfortable as this may be, you have to do this because you want an accusation of this magnitude to be nipped in the bud. It's like turning on the light in a dark room where you think there are creepy crawly things.

Here's why: Say your secretary accuses you of being sexist when you refuse her request to have Friday off to attend a PTA meeting at her child's school. You blow it off as just a fit of annoyance on your secretary's part and mentally make a note to make it up to her with a nice present on the next Administrative Assistants Day.

Only this time, your secretary doesn't keep her annoyance to herself or the other secretaries. She stews on it for a week and then reports it to the human resources department. By the time HR has come to you, you're on the defensive. The whole issue has become very formal, requiring documentation and interviews and more documentation and more interviews. No matter how it's resolved, it goes in your personnel file, you probably end up with a new secretary, and a lot of ill will has been spread.

However, if you are the one to broach the issue first with HR, it would most likely be handled in a different way. Probably, someone from HR would go to your secretary informally, and she would get to express her concerns without it triggering a full-blown formal investigation. HR would give you advice on how to better handle things in the future, your secretary would feel heard while also learning to take care in uttering accusations like that in the first place, and the relationship between you may be a little strained for the short term but not irrevocably fractured.

## Training Helps All

There are many reasons why companies conduct diversity training. Sometimes, it's because employees bring up issues of discrimination. Other times it's because it is good policy to do so regularly. Sometimes the accusations that people make may be so dead-on that a widespread overhaul regarding diversity issues becomes necessary.

If companies are regularly handling their business regarding diversity training—doing it frequently enough to keep it on the minds of employees but not so frequently that people burn out on the concept—then the training will be educational and not just taken as punishment.

Once, I was one of the trainers for a mandatory diversity training given to an entire workforce. Unfortunately, the workshops started right after a very public discrimination lawsuit brought against the institution because of the actions of a high-ranking official. Needless to say, every workshop had someone utter the comment that "it wasn't fair" that they all had to go through diversity training because of a lawsuit brought against one person. Actually, plans for the training had been put in place long before the lawsuit became public knowledge. Also, companies routinely have diversity training requirements for their employees. But these explanations lacked credibility to the employees, who hadn't had diversity training in quite a few years.

Therefore, companies need to check out the best practices for how often diversity training should be held for their industry and their size company, and then they need to commit to having the training. Better yet, companies—whether they're small businesses or in the Fortune 100—should just find ways to incorporate the value of diversity into their business, even if (as a small company) it's just copying articles of interest and leaving them on the break room tables for employees to read.

People generally don't like training on issues they already feel well versed on, but it's important for organizations to communicate that diversity is one of those areas that does not have a concrete bottom of knowledge to reach. It's an ongoing value with changing and evolving issues that workplaces always need to address.

Once upon a time, and even today in many workplace environments, people reduced diversity to literally blacks and whites getting along and teaching men how to not harass women. But mores changes and the laws slowly catch up. For example, until 1964, it was legal for an employer to fire a woman because she announced she was getting married. It's hard for most working adults to wrap their heads around that concept today.

Yet, while actually firing a woman for getting married may be illegal today, companies frequently have to deal with the issues that come up for their female employees. There are more subtle ways those biases creep up about working women and their dedication to work once they get married or start having children. People need to talk about those biases and get training on it.

Depending on the type of business and training, that discussion about working women may have to expand to discussing how a professional woman in an organization has to take into account the cultural nuances of doing business in Arabic countries versus Asian countries versus European countries while the company must not be in violation of U.S. employment laws.

So again, diversity training is never a static, unchanging area that can be hit once and then the employees are good indefinitely. Just as demographics of all kinds ebb and flow, so does understanding.

## Keys to Breaking This Chapter's Code

- When attempting to understand the differences of others, even with the best of intentions, missteps happen.

- Apologizing and asking how you offended someone is a good start for when you've caused an offense. Avoiding name calling and personal labels flung in anger is a good start for when you are the one who has been offended.

- When accusations are made, seek help as an individual. As an organization, consider additional training.

## Diversity Exercise

Simple exercise: This week (or next week if this is Thursday or Friday), find five opportunities to say "I'm sorry."

That's it.

Oh, and not a reflexive "I'm sorry" that comes automatically out of your mouth when you step on someone's toes.

But rather, the conscious, deliberate kind, as in "I did say I would get back to you about that by 10:00 a.m. and here it is 2:30 p.m. and I'm just now getting back to you. I'm sorry."

Five times. Exercise that underused muscle.

# CHAPTER EIGHTEEN

# How Do I Really Call Someone Out on Their Mess When They Have More Rank Than I Do?

*Dear Diversity Diva:*

*I know you're tripping, Miss Diva, if you think that even as a manager I'm going to say squat to upper management about anything important. That man will fire me quicker than I can staple two pieces of paper together and laugh while he's doing it.*

*Signed,*
*Born at Night But Not Last Night*

## Handling Matters with Care

What's the old joke about how you make love to a porcupine? Very carefully. While this is not the funniest joke in the world (or appropriate for the workplace), it's one to keep in mind when deciding if you're going to call out your employer or manager on an issue regarding diversity. Know that it will rarely be well received if you are direct, even if you handle it gently.

Some think that the best way to deal with situations where you have to complain about one of your supervisors is to ignore the problem, but that doesn't remove how the situation affects you. Therefore, you have to evaluate whether it truly is in your best interest to complain or to keep suffering through the issue with your supervisor.

There is no one-size-fits-all rule to decide how to approach it, but in great part, it depends on how the issue personally and directly affects you. Say you believe that your thirty-two-year-old supervisor is discriminating against the people in your department who are over the age of fifty. (The legal threshold for an age discrimination complaint is over the age of forty.) This is just an impression you have from observing whom he picks to promote, whom he has demoted, and how he treats the younger people in the department compared to how he treats the older ones.

Well, since you are in your thirties, it doesn't directly affect you, and you are in a tricky situation because you really don't know enough about the qualifications of the people being promoted or demoted or the reasoning behind why he has picked some people over others. So, in this case, the best thing might be for you to say nothing at all to anyone.

However, let's say you are one of those people over the age of fifty who believes that you have been unfairly passed over for certain jobs when the people selected were a lot younger than you and didn't have your number or level of qualifications. That's when you might want to say something, most likely to someone in the HR department. Once you unleash the issue, however, you can't stuff the genie back into the bottle, so you better be real clear on your allegations with some facts or specific words or behavior to back it up.

If you don't want to go to the HR department because you're not comfortable doing that or view it as being a lot more formal than you want, then you may want to go to another person of authority or power in your workplace. Sometimes that is your boss's boss. However, that route can be one of the riskiest solutions to seek out—as discussed below.

## Playing by the Rules When Handling an Issue

One of the trickiest things to do when you are having a problem with a supervisor or first-line manager is going directly over his or her head to your boss's boss. In some places of employment, there is a structured, formal way of handling problems that may not necessarily burn you. In that instance, this may be a prudent approach because the complaint is done in a way where certain procedures will most likely be followed.

However, if you have the more likely scenario where there is no formalized protocol for approaching a supervisor's supervisor about a problem, you run the very real risk that your complaint will not be treated with the objectivity that is needed. Management tends to back up management when there is an employee complaint or issue. Most managers will tell you differently and it's not always even consciously done, but when one manager is approached by an employee about another manager, the circling of the wagons happens more often than not.

When I was an employment attorney, I almost always represented the companies that got sued, which meant working closely with the managers who were actually accused of what the company was being sued for. Most managers are well meaning, but more often than they want to admit, a manager will put herself in the place of the manager who is accused of something, and thus, she will want to defend her peer's actions. People are human, and defending your own—whatever that is—is natural. Or, the manager may know more back story on what is taking place at a higher leadership level that affected the decisions. Or, the managers have talked about the employee in question, so there is already a built-in bias in place against the employee (or at least the situation).

When there is a problem with a supervisor regarding an issue of diversity, most of the time the best plan is to bring in a third objective person who has as much power over the supervisor as the supervisor has power over you. Usually, that objective third party can best be found by going to the HR department. Also, it is usually best to bring in people as witnesses who have the authority to deal or the experience of dealing with matters like this, so that professional handling of the issues doesn't get muddied and confidentiality is maintained.

With some exceptions, of course, the HR department has a little bit more objectivity about you, your supervisor, or the area of the company where you work. So in going to HR, you have a better chance of getting a full and objective airing of your complaint that doesn't burn you with your boss or the company.

More important, you've cloaked yourself in a little protection by taking it to HR because your issues are on the record, on the off-chance that your supervisor in particular or the company in general decides to take adverse employment action against you in any way. While it may be unlawful to do so, people are human, and humans have a tendency to take it out on other people when they feel they are being unfairly attacked. If the person knows that the complaint has been taken to a higher level or at least brought to the attention of someone outside the area of the company where you both work, then things are more likely to be dealt with in a more professional way that doesn't result in retaliation.

## An Approach That Worked

Sharon, who is a member of an ethnic minority group, sought consultation from me about problems she was having at work that she felt stemmed from her being the only person of color in her department. She believed that she received unfair criticism for her work and that the potential consequences for those problems were disproportionate to how the issues were handled when it came up with others in her department. My role wasn't to determine whether she was correct or incorrect in her assessment but to advise her on the best way to handle a rapidly snowballing situation that could have the end result of derailing her career at that place of employment.

Since Sharon was a professional in a big corporation, I asked her several questions about the company structure, the line of command, etc. I determined that there was a diversity committee and that Hallie, one of the members of that committee, was also a high-ranking member of the department she worked in but was not the direct boss or supervisor of Mary, the primary person Sharon had issues with.

Because of the particular nuances of what Sharon shared with me, I suggested that she initiate a private meeting with Hallie and share her concerns. I stressed to her that she needed to impress on Hallie that she was approaching her because this was an issue of diversity that was having a serious impact on how her competency and reputation were being viewed in the company. Also, I told Sharon that she needed input on how to best handle the situation in a way that addressed the legitimate concerns of Mary, her immediate supervisor, as opposed to the concerns she didn't believe were legitimate.

I also made sure that Sharon knew that she needed to have a better foundation for thinking of this as a diversity issue other than that she and Mary were of different races. She needed to have specific instances and examples of where she felt that diversity—or worse, discrimination—was the real issue.

Sharon had a conversation with Hallie. As a result of the conversation, Hallie set up a three-way meeting between herself, Sharon, and Mary. In that meeting, Mary expressed her legitimate issues about the Sharon's performance. Because of the presence of Hallie—a member of the diversity committee, who was also a respected leader in the department and therefore had details about how both the supervisor *and* the employee should be doing their jobs—Mary kept the issues salient, and Sharon was properly responsive. In other words, with a witness of stature, all of the participants were on their best behavior and the issues stayed narrow and fair.

Sharon followed up with me several months later and told me how much better her job was going and how nipping things in the bud by having the diversity committee member mediate made a huge difference. I was happy for her and how things turned out because it illustrated how good communication and a fair opportunity to be heard are among the best foundations to support diversity in the workplace.

## Keys to Breaking This Chapter's Code

- Addressing issues of diversity where it concerns a direct supervisor requires careful thought on who is best to go to regarding the problems.

- You should approach the option of going directly over your boss's head to his or her boss very carefully.

- Oftentimes, the best resolution of all involves good judgment and creative solutions that allow you and your supervisor to communicate and problem-solve.

## Diversity Exercise

Think of three "honey" ways you can deal with a problem with a supervisor, and also think of three "vinegar" approaches.

As both in- and out-of-the-box examples, "honey" can be things such as taking your boss to lunch where you pay, gifts (if allowed by company policy), a nice e-mail, and joining an affinity group. "Vinegar" approaches could include filing a complaint with HR that you know has no merit, spreading vicious gossip (because, believe it or not, some people do intentionally do this), and sending a nasty e-mail to your boss's boss.

Now examine which (if any) of your ideas are practical and good, which are likely to be effective, and which are likely to be quick and effective career killers.

# CHAPTER NINETEEN

# As a Department Head or Supervisor, How Do I Really Get People Past Conflicts in the Workplace Once They Have Escalated Badly?

*Dear Diversity Diva:*

*Things in my department have gotten bad. Real bad. One race doesn't like another race. An age discrimination suit is on the horizon. Some of the women are making noise about harassment. I just don't know what to do short of firing everyone and starting from scratch with all new employees. What do I do?*

*Signed,*
*Supervising Some Serious . . . Mess*

## The Tipping Point

There are times in the workplace when things reach a decided turning point regarding diversity. It's not really a turning point, sometimes, but a boiling point.

Maybe it's one individual who believes that she is being discriminated against—on the basis of race, gender, sexual orientation, age, or disability. And maybe that one person has filed a complaint and people in the department feel like they are being forced to take sides.

Maybe the one individual is a former employee who has filed a lawsuit for discrimination, and tensions are high as attorneys for the company interview people in the workforce. Also, people are receiving subpoenas to be witnesses in depositions taken by the former employee's attorney. This also raises tensions.

Maybe it's nothing as formal as a lawsuit or even an internal complaint but just several employees who are bonding and banding together over what they see as unfair treatment toward members of the group they are part of.

In any case, there are times in the workplace when the tension bubbles to the point where management needs to deal with it. A point when managers need to stop treating it as a low-grade morale problem and see it for what it is: a powder keg with a long fuse that someone or a group of someones has already lit.

Back in the 1980s, the tagline was "Who you gonna call?" with the answer on everyone's lips being "Ghostbusters!" In the workplace, when things become that ridiculously tense, the answer needs to have that same sense of inevitability. HR is the place to call no matter how difficult it is to make that call.

Or as Martin Luther King Jr. said, "Change does not roll in on the wheels of inevitability, but comes through continuous struggle." In the context of workplace investigations, that's what it seems like until resolution is reached: continuous struggle.

In situations like this, HR should always be brought in so that individual issues can be dealt with easily, or at least immediately and directly. Then, they won't mushroom out of control and turn into a diversity disaster.

## Balanced Investigators

Once things have to be looked into by an investigator, balance—or at least the surface appearance of balance—is important. By balance, I mean having at least two people asking questions of employees. When possible, these investigators should not be the same gender or ethnicity as each other, even if the investigation has nothing to do with gender or race.

That is because you have to give people an option on whom to gravitate toward when you are questioning them about a sticky situation. Some people find it easier opening up to a woman, others to a man. And since there isn't ever a way that you can predict how that comfort level will be determined, it's always best to provide options.

Sometimes you can't provide options, and when that is the case, then you have to roll with it. For example, if the HR investigator scheduled to talk with employees about a diversity situation is a woman and the outside legal counsel sent to the company to help question the employees is also a female, then each employee will have to pick which of the two females he or she has a greater comfort level with.

What I meant about the surface appearance of balance is just that. When people see two women or two men questioning them about an incident, there is a tendency to just lump the questioners together. It doesn't matter if the two women or the two men are as different as a Hawaiian cruise is from an Alaskan snowboarding vacation. It's the same thing with two people of the same ethnicity. But people have a tendency to believe that if they see questioners of two different races, then they have a shot at getting one of the people to see their position more clearly and fairly than the other. It doesn't matter if the fact is totally incorrect. This is the reality when trying to get to the bottom of an issue involving diversity.

As corny as it sounds, when it comes to diversity, people want to see diversity. Mix up the investigators whatever way you can, not to show that you know how to engage in tokenism but to show that diversity is valued in your organization. This also means that if you're going to have two people talking to employees to get to the bottom of an issue, make sure that both investigators have meaningful participation in the conversation. Make sure both people are asking questions or making comments. Plan how to divide up the conversational duties if necessary. The key thing is not to make it look like one investigator is the subservient handmaiden of the other, especially if the one looking like he/she is showing deference to the other would be considered as from a disadvantaged group in the workplace.

## Breeding Grounds for Misunderstanding

One of the issues you have to explore as a manager or diversity leader of any kind is looking at the conversations that you are having or that you are failing to have about diversity that may be creating a breeding ground for misunderstanding.

One example is an employment discrimination case I worked on. The black workers in an organization claimed that when the white supervisor came to work every day, he said good morning to the white employees but not to the black ones. I was one of the attorneys representing the employer. We were unable to determine any evidence one way or another that this supervisor came to work and did this. And frankly, it wasn't germane to the essentials of the lawsuit being brought. However, the perception of these employees was as vivid, as clear, and as unshakable a reality to them as the assuredness they had in spelling their names. There was something in the way the supervisor was conducting himself that created the impression that he was dissing his black employees. Maybe it happened only once, but that one time took on a life of its own. Maybe the white coworkers were people he had worked with longer, and so his "good morning" to them was a little warmer than to the black employees who were newer in the ranks.

Whatever the reason, things like this create a breeding ground for discomfort, disconnection, dissent, and disruption in the workplace. Logic and words have a hard time making an appearance when it comes to how people perceive the actions or interpret the words of others in the workplace whom they choose to place in the category of "different."

It reminds me of my grandmother. In the years that she has had Alzheimer's disease, her mother—who died in 1990—is just as alive and real to her as my mother and I are to her when we visit her at the nursing home. For reasons beyond understanding, the belief in that reality is as true to her as any verifiable fact.

## Diversity Workshops: The Training Wheels of Diversity

People may resent the need for diversity workshops but they are a necessary evil, so to speak. My first book on diversity is titled *Working While Black: A Black Person's Guide to Success in the White Workplace*. While that title has a catchy ring to it, the title that I pitched to the publisher of the book was *Flavor in the Melting Pot*. The reason I preferred my original title is that I found it represented the tone I was trying to create in the advice book I was writing for blacks in the workplace.

To me, society as a whole, and the workplace in particular, is one big old melting pot of flavors and ingredients and spices that create a whole. Separately, the ingredients are good, but together they create an even more outstanding tastiness. But as anyone who has ever cooked anything in a pot with even just a little bit of heat to keep it cooking knows, you have to occasionally take a spoon and stir the pot. This is not to cause chaos in the kitchen but to make sure that nothing is sticking to the bottom of the pot, to make sure that all the flavors are melding, and to make sure there is a fairly even degree of cooking for everything you've put in that pot.

In a nutshell, that's what diversity training is—a way to stir the pot but in a controlled, even-handed way that doesn't end up causing a mess from the contents spewing all over the kitchen.

Diversity training shouldn't be used as a cleanup measure for when things go wrong in the workplace, but as with all rules, there are exceptions. One of those exceptions is having a significant, widespread situation regarding diversity where outsiders can help your workplace get a better grasp on the issues.

## When Outsiders Are a Good Thing

In many ways, a good workplace is like an extended family. And most families, regardless of cultural differences or socioeconomic status, have a deep aversion to "airing dirty laundry" when there is a problem. But sometimes seeking help through an objective mediator is the only way to solve a problem, especially if it is a specific issue between two employees or between an employee and a supervisor and the regular means of resolution are not working. When that is the case, seek outside help since the trust of internal employees may have been breached. If it has gotten particularly bad, have the employees who are involved help with the selection of an outside neutral person.

One of the roles of HR is to determine when that outside neutral person is necessary. Because while it may be tempting to keep escalating problems internal for budgeting and confidentiality reasons, doing so may result in issues continuing to get worse.

## Keys to Breaking This Chapter's Code

- There is almost always a point when a diversity issue goes from being containable and solvable to a problem that tips out of control.

- With investigation issues, it's important to bring as much visible balance and objectivity as possible to generate trust.

- The workplace is a melting pot of difference that always needs to be tended to so that the differences are harmonizing rather than creating a messy stew with clashing flavors.

## Diversity Exercise

If you are a manager, this is an exercise that you should probably do regularly. Research and investigate who can come to your company or department to conduct a good diversity workshop or seminar.

This exercise is important for managers because it is important for you to know the resources you have available to deal with diversity issues, not just when a problem comes up but at all times so that you're not behind the curve.

Many times, in just keeping up regularly on what kind of training is available, while constantly staying vigilant to the issues in your workplace, you may be able to get ahead of the curve in educating your employees.

# CHAPTER TWENTY

# What Is the Purpose of a Company's Annual Diversity Report?

*Dear Diversity Diva:*

*My company has put out a diversity report. It puts one out every year and most of the time I don't bother looking at it. But one day out of boredom, I pulled it up and looked at it and well ... to put it nicely, it seemed like a lot of bull hockey. Why do companies put one out and what's it really supposed to be reporting on?*

*Signed,*
*Worried About the Trees Cut Down for Diversity Reports*

## Why You Need a Diversity Report

Diversity reports are one of those things that big companies and organizations like to put out for several reasons: to make them look like they really are as concerned about diversity as they say they are, to make sure that people whose jobs are devoted to diversity look like they are actually doing some things, and to make themselves look good in the eyes of clients, customers, and potential clients and customers. Also, for the businesses with top leadership that is truly devoted to diversity, the reports provide a marker for not just what they have achieved but for what they hope to do a better job on in the future.

Those reports are sometimes the closest a company gets to a visible, quantifiable, and measurable marker of diversity. It's important and valuable to get the reports down on paper or on a company's computer system. For these reasons, this chapter presents a dissection of a company's diversity report to give you an idea of the various ways of looking at it.

Although the example I'm using here is based on a real company's diversity report, as I have done throughout this book, I'm also going to be careful to not share what this business does. This is not just for confidentiality purposes but also to not distract from the point that this report could be from any company engaged in any industry in the United States. The company is called Widget Makers, Inc. (WMI).

## Publishing a Diversity Report

First of all, WMI gets major points for having an annual diversity report. Not all companies have extensive diversity reports, so an organization that attempts to have some baseline of what it is doing and supplies that information to its employees and the public provides a starting point for someone who has questions.

Like a publicly held company that makes public information on its financial details and spending, a company, at least on the surface, shows a degree of openness and integrity when it addresses diversity.

## Timing

Doing it annually makes sense if the main point of the report is to summarize accomplishments, since doing it every year provides a baseline of a significant period of time having passed to compare how the company has improved and grown its diversity initiatives.

However, if the company is trying to show that diversity is more than just a rote, fill-in-the-blank agenda item on its public relations "to do" list, then a quarterly report might be better timing. Even if a company still wants to do a larger, more extensive annual report, publishing a report quarterly shows that diversity is an ongoing commitment.

## Vision Statement

WMI gives a nice broad vision statement on what diversity means to the organization in terms of describing the company as a place where every employee is respected, treated fairly, etc. However, WMI fails to show how that fits into the bigger picture of the organization. Does diversity help WMI attract new business? Is it a mandate for keeping existing business? Is this a big push in the industry that WMI belongs to, and if so, is WMI measuring up?

Companies are crystal clear in communicating how changes, policies, and standards impact the bottom line when it comes to profit, and diversity needs to be treated the same way. The report should indicate how the vision for diversity fits into the larger vision statement of WMI.

## Diversity Committee

It's admirable that WMI has a diversity committee and that it's primarily the committee that puts together the annual report with oversight and input from WMI's top management. And it's great that this annual report lists who is on the committee. However, the problem is that WMI's diversity committee is a little top-heavy. Now, on the one hand, WMI pats itself on the back for the top-down commitment that it makes to diversity. However, more than half of the fairly large committee consists of managers, from mid-managers to top management. WMI thinks that this communicates, "We take diversity seriously! This is such an important issue that we want to show that this isn't just something we delegate to the little guys!"

True, that is part of what WMI is communicating. But very few of its committee members are from the rank and file (once you subtract managers and members of the committee who are from the HR department). So do you really have a committee that is indicating a sincere commitment to diversity, where you have enough people intimately involved with the issues to give you meaningful feedback and areas to address? Most employees looking at the list of members will probably not feel that the committee represents any interests of theirs, but rather that the company just wants to *look* like it is representing the interests of the workforce.

## Self-Graded Report Card

WMI grades itself on how it feels that it has achieved its diversity goals. The good part of that is that WMI clearly expresses goals that it is rating itself on. That's a plus because it's only in knowing what you are being graded on that you know whether you are making progress. And WMI doesn't give itself A+ grades in everything. WMI acknowledges that it has work to do.

However, grading yourself is sort of like, well, grading yourself. I'm sure all sixteen-year-olds who take a driving test would probably give themselves high marks and an automatic driver's license no matter how many questions they missed on the written test and how many other cars they "just side-swiped a little." Rating yourself on anything is always tricky, which is why an employee survey to supplement the self-grading might be a good plan.

## Showing the Numbers

Frankly, this is one of the areas that I think most company diversity reports fail the most miserably at. They report the number of women and minorities as if these are the only two numbers worthy of reporting. Now, granted, those are huge areas, but they are far from being the only numbers that are important.

For example, WMI's report has only the most general categories of numbers: male members in management, female members in management, minority members in management, and minority members not in management.

So let's go over what this does not address. First of all, it doesn't break down how "minorities" are being defined. Are we just talking racial minorities? Are we including national origin or people with disabilities or members of the GLBT community? Even if we are just talking racial, where are the specific numbers for blacks, Hispanics, Asians, and Native Americans? My point isn't that a diversity report should divulge all these numbers—just that if you're going to make blanket statements, define what your blanket covers.

Second, if you're going to address the issue of females and you are going to address the issue of minorities (even if you don't identify how you are defining minorities), then you need to operate in full disclosure and break it down further by saying how many minority females are in management. You need to compare this to the number of minority males and to the total number of people in management. In other words, to quote from the song "Confessions" by R&B singer Usher, "If I'm gonna tell it, then I gotta tell it all."

Also, one of the reasons to me that most reporting of diversity numbers fails to reveal anything significant is that even when the company is specific in its breakdown of numbers, rarely do the numbers reflect turnover and retention, which are key to telling anything about the numbers. That's because while many companies have become masters at recruiting, it's retention that tells the story of how well diversity is really working when it comes to certain groups.

The other missing number—which is something you will almost never see in any diversity report—is a general idea of how many complaints the company has received on the basis of diversity issues, including how many got resolved or are pending resolution.

For example, in fiscal year 2008 alone, the EEOC received 19,453 complaints under the Americans with Disabilities Act of 1990 (ADA), with 16,705 of those complaints considered by the EEOC to be resolved. What are the chances that the average company, in its annual diversity report, will list its individual share of that slice of diversity statistics? Arguably, there could be confidentiality issues with that disclosure in even the most sweeping terms, but it might be worth addressing in the report.

## Diversity Programs

In WMI's diversity report, it is of interest that there is a section that lists the company's participation in various diversity programs. This includes hosting and participating in job fairs and scholarship programs, working with other companies on diversity, working with the industry on diversity, and having mentoring programs for both high school and college students.

However, the key word in the above paragraph is the word "participation." While attending and getting involved in various diversity initiatives is admirable—and WMI is to be commended for that because not all companies do so—the report fails to reflect how much of that participation is converted to actual hires or even interviews. Understandably, specific names shouldn't be mentioned so as not to put an uncomfortable and personal spotlight on individual employees, but it would be telling to be able to report that five people from minority groups from the Widget Industry Job Fair at Mojo University interviewed with WMI in the past year.

## Customer/Client Information

Of course, WMI is going to spend a great deal of time reporting on the customer and client partnerships it was involved in on the issue of diversity—several full pages worth. But to the average employee or potential employee looking at that list, it just looks like free advertising for the people who keep them in business. Also, it ends up looking like more self-congratulatory puffing that all the respective parties can use to enhance their own "street cred" on the issue of diversity. It's a corporate version of the following: "Oh my God, I love your haircut!" "Thanks, I love that shirt you're wearing!" "This old thing? No, it's your shirt that is absolutely stunning."

Anyone who has ever listened to a conversational exchange like this knows this is just mutual bragging disguised as mutual complimenting. While there is nothing wrong with an annual diversity report being used in part as a marketing tool, it's important that companies make sure that the report is more of a genuine reporting of what takes place with diversity in their company than a glossy PR piece.

## Awards

The next section addresses a list of the awards relating to diversity that WMI has received in the last year. The reason for that list is self-explanatory. It makes the company look really, really good. After all, if media organizations, groups specializing in diversity initiatives, respected advocacy groups, and national representatives of the company's own industry keep giving WMI awards for diversity efforts, then that must mean that WMI is doing everything right and is above reproach in all things diversity, right?

On the surface, that's true. Awards of this nature are given to companies that do make a pronounced effort to spend time and money promoting and supporting diversity efforts. Some of those awards are well-deserved reflections of the credit that many companies should receive for their efforts and accomplishments.

But those awards tend to be given to companies that put themselves in position to be nominated for these awards. Also, it's not a coincidence that on a lot of the national lists for best companies to work at for fill-in-the-blank category of employees, you tend to see the same big national corporate names over and over again because the bigger the corporation, the bigger the machinery it has behind making sure that it is creating the right public impression on that topic.

Whenever I see these lists come out or see that a company has received an award for creating a particularly good working environment for a specific group of people, my personal concern is hoping that it doesn't artificially and unfairly raise the bar higher for any individual members of the group who bring up a legitimate issue about a diversity or discrimination challenge that they may have.

## Community Involvement

The next part of WMI's report, which is one of the longest sections, lists company involvement during the past year in a number of events, discussions, contributions, and donations to or about anything even remotely related to diversity locally and nationally.

While everything listed may be factually correct, there are a couple of ways of looking at lists like this. From the standpoint of the company leadership, it's an example of "See, look how much time we're taking away from our business to throw time, money, and employee involvement toward this diversity stuff! We take diversity seriously!" And of course, it is a sign that leadership does take diversity seriously, but it's still about externals. It's about doing the things where WMI has its name on the banner, in the brochure, in the media coverage.

Community involvement with diversity does help in recruiting and does provide many "feel good" moments for employees who think those things are important. Most important, to the groups and the issues that are being served by WMI's contributions, the support that WMI and other companies give to their endeavors means everything. But for the employees of WMI, it just might not be the whole story.

## The Bottom Line on Diversity Reports

It probably sounds like I'm bashing annual diversity reports. I am a little. Not because there is anything intrinsically wrong with them but because the content can seem shallow and hollow—in some cases, downright manufactured—to the employees who are actually living diversity issues in the workplace.

What if I'm sitting beside an older Hispanic female coworker who has had to resort to an official HR complaint because she has been passed over three times for a better position that she is overqualified for, while she simultaneously has to help train the young white males who get picked for the position? If that's the case, then reading about the award my company has received from a local Hispanic organization for its involvement in community issues is going to make my stomach turn a little bit.

If I've observed how many times my pregnant coworkers have had to deal with outright hostility from our supervisor whenever a maternity leave has to be scheduled, I may laugh out loud when I see the company e-mail seeking volunteers to attend an event where the company will receive an award from a prominent local women's group for being one of the best employers in the city for working women.

The examples could go on and on but they add up to the same thing: Loud expressions of commitment to diversity, along with a battalion of crystal awards for diversity efforts, mean that employees will hold the company to high standards of integrity.

And trust me: No company wants to have a large contingent of its employees out in the community saying that the company's reputation for being great in diversity is one Big Corporate Lie.

Every company—especially the ones that receive a lot of attention for their diversity initiatives—wants to make it a high priority to make sure that the attention is warranted.

Remember, every one of the thousands of people who filed an employment discrimination complaint with the EEOC works for some company. And some of those companies published a glossy annual diversity report along with receiving awards for their great diversity efforts in the year that individual charges were filed.

## Keys to Breaking This Chapter's Code

- It can be a positive, transparent move for a company to publish an annual diversity report to help it make progress on its diversity initiatives.

- But it is important that a company examines whether reporting on a few numbers is really a good indicator of its progress.

- Companies might be better served in asking the people who actually work for them to grade them on their diversity efforts so that their reports don't merely look like glossy advertisements for how they want diversity to look to outsiders.

## Diversity Exercise

See if your company has an annual diversity report. Print it out. Grab a pen. Read the report. Underline the parts that interest you or that you have questions about and then go ask someone.

For as long as you work at the company, it's your business too.

# CHAPTER TWENTY-ONE

# As a Company, When Do We Know When We Have Actually Achieved Diversity?

*Dear Diversity Diva:*

*My company goes on and on and on about diversity. We got African-Americans, we got Mexican-Americans, we got Asian-Americans, we got deaf folks, we got gay folks. I mean, we're good. Why do we have to keep doing stuff?*

*Signed,*
*Done with Dealing with Diversity*

## Is There an End Point?

Is there a point when diversity is achieved? It's a good question and not one that is easily answered. To me, the simple answer is no, but a good company can have high marks when it comes to diversity and be well positioned to keep those high marks.

Also, just like one would never think there is an end point to safety issues or the fiscal soundness of a company, diversity has to be seen in that category of work priorities that require constant vigilance.

The reason that it can't ever be totally achieved is because diversity is about change and balancing different demographics. Demographics shift. Suppose you have a delectable workplace where there is a balance of races, distributed evenly throughout management; people with disabilities who have perfect access to the entire building and every reasonable accommodation made; different generations of employees mixing well; and a fair representation of class, religion, sexual orientation, and all other groups.

Until ....

A new secretary starts work. She is a Muslim and adheres to wearing traditional Islamic garb as well as having most of the month of August off for Ramadan. Oh yeah, and she needs to have time to get her required number of prayers in during the workday, even though this gives her more break time than the other secretaries and the timing of her breaks doesn't fit in with the regular break schedule.

Other secretaries are upset. The bosses of the other secretaries are upset because it impacts their work. Suddenly, the self-congratulatory back patting that the company has been giving itself for its great diversity efforts isn't so easy to do anymore.

Yes, diversity at that particular self-proclaimed diversity mecca isn't quite so great anymore. Especially when the word "mecca" in such a flip context now offends a specific employee.

## Numbers Don't Lie, or Do They?

Every company or organization that is large and organized enough to have an HR division keeps numbers on at least a few of the demographics of its workforce—typically race and gender. Sometimes, all those figures do is show the numbers of people who work at the organization. Some organizations may break the numbers down by category of workers, especially if it is a company that has been involved in one or more employment lawsuits or is in an industry that has a big push for diversity.

But even if a company keeps track of the racial background of its employees, for example, what story about the company regarding race does this really tell?

Just for starters, do the numbers answer the following questions:

- Do the numbers compare the demographics of the company with the metropolitan area where the company is located?

- Do the numbers indicate the ethnicity of the people who have applied for jobs at the company but were turned down?

- Do the numbers break down the numbers of people in management of a particular ethnicity versus the employees of that race who are not in management?

- Do the numbers reflect in any way the retention rate of employees by race over a period of time?

I'm going to break down the importance of these questions to indicate how numbers regarding diversity in the workplace could be a little deceptive, even when the company doesn't mean to be.

My first question—how the demographics of the company compare to the metropolitan area where the company is located—goes to the issue of whether the company racially represents, at least roughly, the demographics of the hiring pool. Obviously, that will not always be a direct match. For example, if a company specializes in computer technology and 80 percent of the people who work there have degrees in computer science or something related, then the racial demographics of the city or town that the company is in will not bear a lot of direct relation. However, if a company's main workforce is employed in a call center that takes calls from customers, the level of education bears much lesser correlation to who holds the jobs. But if there is a huge difference in the population percentage of a certain ethnic group compared to that group's proportion in the workplace, then it might be another matter. The demographics of the call center employees should roughly match those of the area where the company is located.

The second question—regarding the number of applicants by race for a job—is telling because it also goes to getting a better indication of whether the company's numbers look so good after all. For example, let's say that a company in Texas has a facility located between Austin and San Antonio, and 35 percent of its workforce is Hispanic, which is roughly the same percentage of Hispanics who live in the area. On the surface, depending on your point of view, that might appear to be a good number. But what if only 25 percent of the Hispanics who make it to a finalist position for a job are hired versus 65 percent of the Caucasian applicants who make it to a finalist interview? Then the numbers—and the reasons behind them—deserve another look.

The third question—comparing the percentage of people of a particular ethnicity who are in management with those who are not in management—is probably more obvious in its point. If a hospital has really high numbers of black and Hispanic employees, for example, but the bulk of the number comes from the cleaning and cooking staff, is that hospital doing better when it comes to the hiring of medical staff than one that has a far lower total number of minorities but far more minority nurses, doctors, and other medical professionals?

The fourth question is really the heart of whether the numbers are real or not. It's the issue of retention. Let's say a medium-size company says that 12 percent of its workforce is black, and that 12 percent translates to thirty-eight employees and reflects the community demographics. Without looking at it in terms of retention, that number looks fair, right? If you pull a copy of the same company's numbers from five years before and the numbers and percentage are roughly the same, then the company is really looking good, isn't it?

But what if you compared the names of those employees from five years ago to the names of the blacks in the current report and find out that only ten of those black employees are in both reports? That gives you a turnover rate for blacks of more than three times the average retention rate for the entire company, which is about 80 percent. Those numbers don't have the same pretty bow around them, do they?

## Do You Know How to Party?

Every workplace is different when it comes to the environment it provides for its employees to work in. Some are straight, "no chaser" type of places where people come to work, the workstations are comfortable but not fancy, the company closes for the major national holidays, and maybe there is one big annual company event like a summer picnic or a winter holiday party. Many companies, on the other hand, like to provide lots of bells and whistles for the employee experience. Some businesses even have an entire department of people whose entire existence consists of thinking of ways to enhance the lives of employees by making work fun.

With the companies that make the effort to give employees an enhanced experience, where comfort and fun is a priority and where they don't mind putting it in the budget to do so, events celebrating diversity can have a big impact.

However, these events shouldn't be the only way that a company honors diversity. If a company slaps up a few Black History Month posters, has a Cinco de Mayo buffet, and passes out some Chinese New Year fortune cookies, that may be cute and even enjoyable, but it's not very educational.

My point is not that companies should not do these things but that they should provide context so that all employees have the opportunity to learn why the company is going through the trouble of doing any of this. Otherwise, it smacks of tokenism.

For example, if you are going to have a free Cinco de Mayo luncheon for your employees, that is a very nice gesture. It really is. There aren't too many people who wouldn't line up for free tacos. But if, as a company, you don't attempt to pass out or post information about the history of Cinco de Mayo, or maybe even have a little program over the lunch hour where people can discuss diversity issues while they are noshing on their tacos, then you might as well be serving hamburgers and fries.

Have these diversity events—please have them—but have them as an expression of your company value system by explaining why you are having them.

## Can Your Employers See Through You?

One of the big words in recent years in the corporate context is the issue of transparency. This is the concept of how open and accessible a company makes its business so that employees, shareholders, and the public feel that the company is operating with honesty and integrity. After the numerous corporate meltdowns that bilked people of their retirement funds, everyone believes that honest companies are a good thing.

Typically, however, issues of diversity are not what people are talking about when the issue of transparency comes up, but it is another area where companies could stand to be a little more forthcoming. For example, the racial composition and number of employees, while not a secret, isn't a thing that many companies publicize to their employees for a variety of reasons.

## Evaluating the Evaluations

Another way a company can determine whether it is even close to having true diversity that works is to have someone periodically check the organization's written job evaluations to determine if there is consistency and fairness in how employees are treated.

For example, if in doing an evaluation of the evaluations, there emerges a noticeable tendency to comment on the personal appearance of women (even if it is in terms of discussing their professional demeanor) far more disproportionately to commenting on that matter with men, then that is an issue. Similarly, if the "attitude" of minority employees (even when positive) is mentioned frequently in their evaluations while only the work itself is addressed in the evaluations of white employees (except in extreme cases), then that too is a problem that needs to be addressed.

This may not be a quantifiable way of evaluating the effectiveness of your diversity IQ, so to speak, at your company, but it's a valid one because employees talk. You can make them sign every confidentiality form in the world, but they talk. They especially talk when they are ticked about what they hear. And you know the number one thing that employees compare stories on when they are talking about their evaluations? You got it: why some things were addressed in one person's evaluation versus those exact same issues not being addressed in someone else's evaluation.

How you evaluate your employees is a key indicator of how your company is really doing regarding diversity.

## Complaints as an Area to Grade

A fairly obvious standard to use to grade how well a company has achieved diversity is to determine how it rates on the number of complaints brought against the company, which includes employee complaints based on diversity issues.

There will never be a company that can say that no employees have ever had issues based on feeling that they were treated differently because of their membership in a group. If a company is large enough, there will always be people who have issues.

The number and severity of the issues is one of the signs that a company has not grasped diversity as well as it should. If a company is hit with discrimination suit after discrimination suit, with a few class actions thrown in for good measure, that's a sign that the company has work to do. However, if the number and severity of those lawsuits was a long time in the company's past—say, fifteen to twenty years ago—it may mean that the company has evolved to having high diversity marks today as a result of lessons learned and the philosophical and political structure the company had to dismantle to build anew.

Which leads to the other issue about complaints: How are they resolved? Does a company have a history and pattern of handling issues of diversity and discrimination promptly, fairly, efficiently, and confidently, with no retaliation against the complaining employee or set of employees? Or does a company leave resolution of diversity issues to confidential settlements that cause complaining employees to "disappear"?

When a diversity bad apple finds its way in the company's structure after full and fair investigation, is that bad apple rooted out with all the damage caused addressed and remedied by the leadership? If so, that is an organization on the road to getting high marks for diversity.

## Change a Gonna Come

Ultimately, a company can no more permanently achieve diversity than anyone can ever permanently achieve a perfect safety record that never has to be reexamined. But a company can set in place systems, structure, values, carrots, and sticks and work to make sure that it deals well with the changing differences and changing circumstances that will always hit an organization.

The only real achievement in workplace diversity is keeping it as a value that always requires attention and intention.

## Keys to Breaking This Chapter's Code

- There is no end point to a company's dealing with diversity because there is always some evolving issue of diversity for an organization to handle.

- Numbers regarding diversity in the workplace are only a starting point for determining whether a company truly has a good handle on diversity.

- A company can do fun things to honor diversity, but at the end of the day it's the substantive issues like widespread complaints and failure to deal with ongoing issues that tell the real story.

## Diversity Exercise

Go back over the previous exercises in this book and decide if your perspective has changed enough to do some of them again.

Hopefully, the answer you give requires you to do just that.

Diversity always evolves and changes. Hopefully, your perspectives do the same.

# CONCLUSION

In an ideal world, I would have written the perfect book on diversity in the workplace—a book that leads to everyone in the workplace getting along great, finding joy in the differences of others, gaining wisdom from what they learn from others, and truly being able to shine as the best employees they can be because all they ever really had to worry about was doing their job, doing it well, and finding opportunities to grow.

A book that led to a workplace like that might even get me a Nobel Peace Prize, because a country full of happy, productive workers would probably lead to a more peaceful country.

But I'm pragmatic and humble enough to just hope that this book leads to readers thinking about diversity in a more expansive, accessible way. A way for all managers to create better workspaces and workplaces for themselves, the people they work with, and the intertwined global workplace community.

Thank you for giving me the chance to do that.

Michelle@MichelleTJohnson.com

# INDEX